CITY OF VICTORY

City of Victory

VIJAYANAGARA

THE MEDIEVAL HINDU CAPITAL
OF SOUTHERN INDIA
PHOTOGRAPHS BY JOHN GOLLINGS
ESSAY AND SITE DESCRIPTIONS BY
JOHN M. FRITZ AND GEORGE MICHELL

APERTURE

King and Capital
I saw that it was a city of enormous magnitude and population, with a king of
perfect rule and hegemony whose kingdom stretched . . . more than a thousand
leagues. Most of his regions were flourishing, and he possessed around three
hundred ports. He had a thousand elephants with bodies like mountains and miens
like demons. The city of Vijayanagara . . . has no equal in the world.
ABDUL RAZZAQ, Persian visitor to Vijayanagara, 1443

PUBLISHED WITH THE ASSISTANCE OF THE GETTY GRANT PROGRAM. APERTURE GRATEFULLY ACKNOWLEDGES ITS SUPPORT.

Composition by Fisher Composition, Inc., New York. Printed and bound in Germany by H. Stürtz AG in Würzburg.

Library of Congress Catalog Number: 90-084834
Hardcover ISBN: 0-89381-467-9

Aperture Foundation, Inc. publishes a periodical, books, and portfolios of fine photography to communicate with serious photographers and creative people everywhere. A complete catalog is available upon request. Address: 20 East 23 Street, New York, New York 10010.

Citations: Abdul Razzaq, see W.M. Thackston, *A Century of Princes: Sources on Timurid History and Art*, Cambridge, Mass., 1989, p. 307; Domingo Paes and Fernao Nuniz, see R. Sewell, *A Forgotten Empire*, London, 1900, pp. 254-259, 261,270-274, 371; Ramayana, see W. Buck, *Ramayana*, Berkeley and Los Angeles, 1976, pp. 345-348; Rayavachakamu, see P. Wagoner, *Tidings of the King: An Account of Krishnadevaraya of Vijayanagaram Translated from the Telugu Rayavachakamu*; Duarte Barbosa, see M.L. Dames, *The Book of Duarte Barbosa*, London, 1918, I, pp. 201-202.

The quotation from the Ramayana (pp. 30-31) is with the permission of the University of California Press. Phillip Wagoner has agreed to the reproduction of a small extract from his Rayavachakamu manuscript (p. 62). The plan of the Vithala temple complex (p. 93) is with the kind permission of Pierre-Sylvain and Vasundhara Filliozat.

———————

The staff at Aperture for *City of Victory: Vijayanagara, the Medieval Hindu Capital of Southern India* is Michael E. Hoffman, Executive Director; Andrew Wilkes, Editor; Jane Marsching, Assistant Editor; Susannah Levy, Editorial Work-Scholar; Stevan Baron, Production Director; Linda Tarack, Production Associate.

Book design by: Wendy Byrne

Endpapers: Courtly processions and hunting scenes carved on the sides of the multistoried platform in the royal center.

Title Page: (1) Distant view of the Vithala temple complex on the bank of the Tungabhadra river in the sacred center; Matanga Hill is in the distance.

Opposite: (2) Mandalas of miniature lingas on boulders beside the Tungabhadra River.

TABLE OF CONTENTS

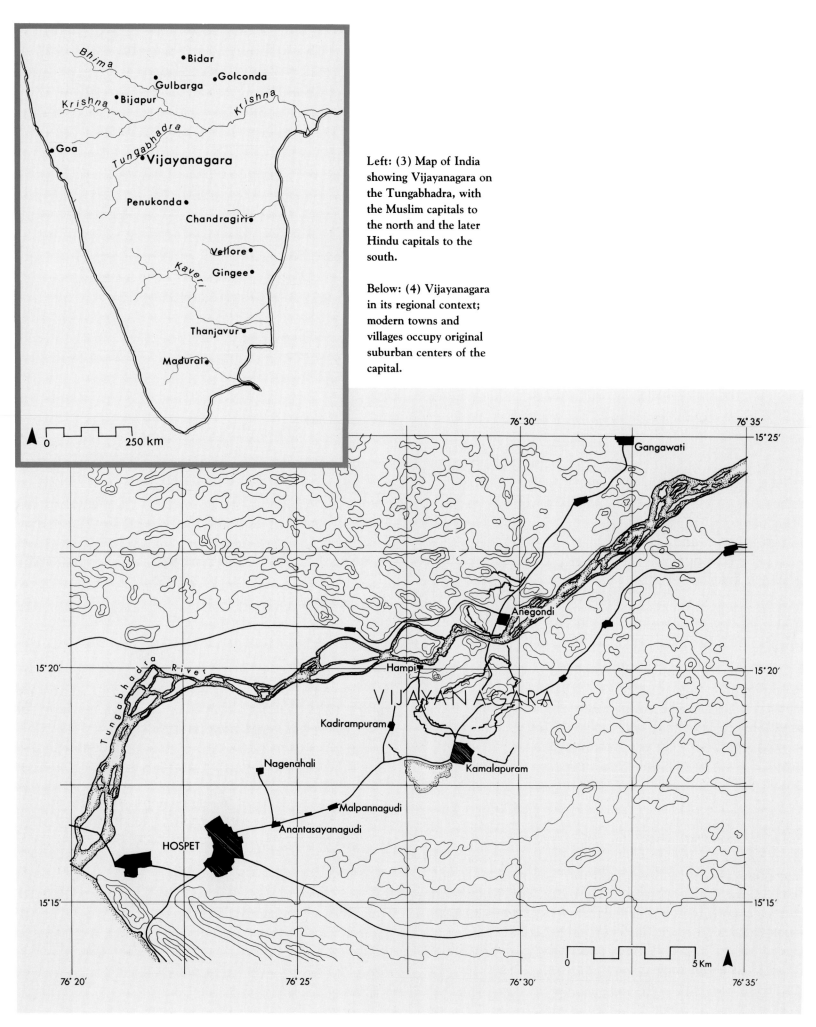

Left: (3) Map of India showing Vijayanagara on the Tungabhadra, with the Muslim capitals to the north and the later Hindu capitals to the south.

Below: (4) Vijayanagara in its regional context; modern towns and villages occupy original suburban centers of the capital.

PREFACE

Vijayanagara, City of Victory, was the capital of the vast Hindu empire in southern India that flourished from the middle of the fourteenth century until 1565, when it was sacked and destroyed by Muslim armies. The city never recovered from this onslaught, and its ruins have been decaying for more than four hundred years. While Vijayanagara's importance in Indian history is considerable, comparatively few historians and archaeologists are personally acquainted with the site. Those who do make the journey to Vijayanagara's ruins, however, whether scholars, pilgrims, or tourists, are amazed and delighted to discover how much survives of the city's former glory.

Unlike the capitals of earlier Hindu kingdoms in India, which have generally vanished from view except for their religious monuments, Vijayanagara preserves a significant range of civic and residential buildings. These standing and ruined monuments are set within a remarkable landscape of granite hills that serves as a natural fortress. But Vijayanagara is also a constructed citadel complete with massive walls, gateways, and watchtowers. Within the city are palaces, courtly pavilions, ceremonial platforms, stables, and stores maintained by a sophisticated water system. There are innumerable temples and shrines dedicated to different Hindu cults and some to Jain saviors. Sculptures and paintings adorn these buildings, illustrating mythological and royal themes.

The grand scale of the capital attests to the resources available to the Vijayanagara kings. The diverse styles of military, civic, courtly, and religious buildings express the cosmopolitan character of urban life and the rich artistic traditions patronized by the city's elite population. Yet not all of Vijayanagara's material record is immediately visible. Foundations of buildings and fragments of portable artifacts such as pottery lie buried in the soil that has accumulated since the destruction of the capital. Together with these remains, the monuments of Vijayanagara provide a substantial picture of a Hindu royal capital. The forms and locations of broken pottery and metal and glass objects yield clues about the inhabitants of Vijayanagara and their occupations. The historical records of the period permit these buildings and artifacts to be interpreted within the context of an elaborate courtly life.

Vijayanagara's ancient remains constitute a fragile heritage. Many buildings are threatened by collapse; others are being modified by local inhabitants who do not appreciate their value for understanding the past. Buried remains are being destroyed by irrigation, farming, and construction, all of which alter the land surface. Though Vijayanagara has now been added to UNESCO's World Heritage List of ancient places of global significance, the site still awaits a master plan for conservation that will guarantee it adequate protection.

The international team whose work at Vijayanagara is presented in this volume is undertaking an architectural documentation of standing and ruined structures, as well as an archaeological reconnaissance of surface features and artifacts. This thorough examination of Vijayanagara's visible remains is contributing to knowledge about the site and to a new interpretation of its monuments. But this study also aims to attract the attention of a general audience. The magnificent black-and-white photographs by John Gollings give the best possible idea of the Vijayanagara monuments in their natural setting by communicating the imposing quality of the buildings and the inventiveness of their compositions.

The accompanying text by John M. Fritz and George Michell is divided into two parts. The introduction at the beginning of the volume presents the historical, cultural, and religious context of the monuments. It emphasizes Vijayanagara as an imperial capital, residence of an immensely powerful dynasty, and the focus of the largest and wealthiest empire of southern India. The comprehensive description of monuments in the different zones of the city which follows is illustrated with maps, architectural drawings, and photographs. The appendices give a dynastic table of the Vijayanagara kings, and glossaries of architectural terms and Indian names. The bibliography lists the most important publications on the subject.

ACKNOWLEDGMENTS

Since 1980, when we began work at Vijayanagara, we have benefited from the assistance of a large number of volunteer professionals and students from Australia, Great Britain, India, and the United States. This team has been composed of archaeologists, architects, art historians, and epigraphists. Other scholars, too, have visited the site to contribute their own expertise. Permission to document the Vijayanagara monuments was kindly granted by the Government of India (Department of Education) and the Archaeological Survey of India. Accommodation at the site, including facilities for a drawing office and an excellent kitchen, was generously made available by the Government of Karnataka Department of Archaeology and Museums. Without the personal interest and collaboration of the director, Dr. M. S. Nagaraja Rao, and his staff, the international team would have been unable to stay at the site. The costs of fieldwork were covered by grants from the British Academy, the Asian Cultural Council, and the Special Foreign Currency Program of the Smithsonian Institution administered by the American Institute of Indian Studies. Many members of the international team have made a substantial contribution over the years by paying their own travel expenses.

Preparation and analysis of data collected in the field were funded by the National Endowment for the Humanities, the National Science Foundation, the Society for South Asian Studies, and several private donors. The Arthur M. Sackler Gallery, Smithsonian Institution, Washington, D. C., in association with the Rockefeller Foundation, kindly provided a home for the Vijayanagara project in 1988–89. The manuscript for this volume was written in Washington during this period, with editorial assistance by Janice Bailey-Goldschmidt and valuable criticisms and suggestions by Anila Verghese and Phillip Wagoner.

We wish to acknowledge a special debt to the photographer John Gollings, with whom we shared the excitement of discovering Vijayanagara. As his photographs vividly demonstrate, Gollings's vision of the monuments in their natural setting adds immeasurably to the impact of this superb site.

Without the initial enthusiasm of Steve Dietz at Aperture, we would not have been compelled to work on the text. A generous grant from the J. Paul Getty Trust in 1989 made this handsome volume a possibility. Production schedules have been expertly supervised by Susan Coliton and her staff; the elegant design is by Wendy Byrne.

To all of these institutions and individuals we are truly grateful. None, however, is responsible for the opinions expressed here.

JOHN M. FRITZ AND GEORGE MICHELL

My first season on the site was a humbling experience even though I was an experienced architectural photographer. After an initial walk around the site, I had the luxury of a whole month to photograph fifty or so major monuments. Eight years later, a wiser photographer, I was beginning to understand the dimension of my error. A thorough photographic documentation required a yearly team of photographers, all volunteers from India, Australia, and Italy. In arduous heat, these assistants willingly labored stone by stone, recording every major building and sculpture in detail. I thank them all: Snehal Shah, Raimonda Buitoni, Dee Foster, Rob Colvin, Polly Borland, Peter White, and my wife, Kate Gollings. My local guide, Virayya, interpreter, nurse, and comic, taught me lessons in humanity not easily gained in the West. Dr. M. S. Nagaraja Rao, C. S. Patil, and Balasubramanya built darkrooms at the campsite and instructed me in archaeology during memorable evenings of food and companionship.

Most of the photographs were made with a Linhof Technika on 4″ x 5″ film and lit with a Balcar portable flash. Both camera and flash were horribly abused but never failed. Equally reliable was the trusty Indian Ambassador car, with U. Srinivas as driver, without whom our task would have been much more difficult.

JOHN GOLLINGS

**(5) Zones of
Vijayanagara showing
sacred center on the
Tungabhadra,
intermediate irrigated
valley, fortified urban
core, and royal center.**

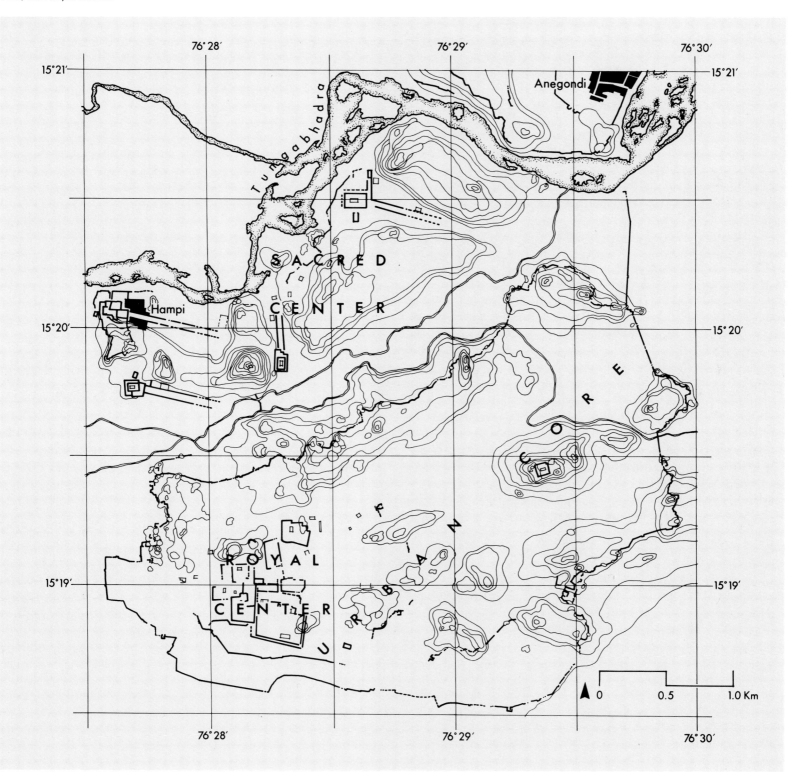

WHERE KINGS AND GODS MEET

L ike other ancient sites where human destinies are inseparable from myth, Vijayanagara cannot be fully comprehended in terms of mere historical and archaeological facts. For more than two hundred years, the city fulfilled the military, administrative, and residential needs of ruler and court while performing a much more important function as capital of a Hindu empire. Indeed, Vijayanagara was the urban realization of cosmological principles which infused the ruler with divine power. When political and military success combined with sacred authority, the king and his capital came to have an epic, almost mythical, dimension.

In India, the worlds of kings and gods are not separate domains; on the contrary, rulers become transcendent figures, while deities are treated as regal personalities. This fluid boundary between divine and royal realms is a dominant theme at Vijayanagara. It is part of the symbolic system which gives meaning to the layout of the city and its monuments as well as to the relationship between buildings and the landscape which envelops them. This symbolic system can be comprehended only within a framework of Hindu myth and culture.

Hinduism incorporates a larger part of Indian thought and action than is communicated by the Western notion of "religion." It is a synthesis of many different beliefs, practices, and modes of living and thinking, all bound together in a distinctive cultural continuity. A feature of this cohesive force is that religious and nonreligious matters are never separate; it is unimaginable that any activity, impulse, or process is without some connection with the divine. Hinduism encompasses the complete spectrum of Indian life, from the everyday agricultural labors of the villager to the transcendental speculations of the philosopher. The ruler in his capital, concerned with the display of military prowess, ceremonial public appearances, and pleasurable pursuits, is also an essential component in this scheme. Architecture, too, is embraced by the Hindu view of life. Temples, palaces, and royal cities serve the everyday requirements of religious and courtly rituals, but they also form part of a complex symbolic system which embodies the most elevated notions of Hindu philosophy.

We may derive knowledge about Hindu symbolic systems in India from a number of sources. For royal cities, bodies of theoretical literature known as shastras have existed for more than two thousand years. These ancient Sanskrit texts are manuals for the proper construction of sacred and secular monuments. They codify the layouts of capital cities, defining the appropriate spatial framework

(6) **Tungabhadra Valley from the two-storied gateway above the Narasimha temple; distant view of the Virupaksha temple complex at Hampi.**

Above: (7) Ruined structures lining steps on the northern slope of Matanga Hill, highest point in the sacred center.

Below: (8) Ruined watchtowers guarding the fort of Anegondi, which continued to be used after the sack of Vijayanagara.

Above: (9) Gateway at the summit of Hemakuta Hill, on a path leading down to Hampi past the oldest temples at the site.

Below: (10) Rock-cut images of Nandi and Ganesha on boulders beside the Tungabhadra express the river's sanctity.

in which kings and gods may meet. Such theoretical models create urban images for the perfect Hindu society. They prescribe the distribution of all social groups within ideal royal cities, locating the ruler at or near the center of his capital. All around, arranged in concentric rings or squares, are the different classes of Hindu society. The higher ranks are closer to the center; the lower ranks are further outside. This spatial ordering of the human world always refers to a central god.

The regulating model for royal Hindu cities in India is the mandala, the geometric pattern which represents the order of the universe. Mandala designs are oriented according to the cardinal directions and in harmony with the movement of heavenly bodies such as the sun, moon, and planets. Cosmic order is thereby incorporated into the plan of the mandala. Divinities, too, are accommodated, since most mandalas have concentric schemes of squares or rings, each the "seat" of an important god. The creator of the Hindu universe, Brahma, is generally situated in the center, at the highest and most powerful point of the diagram. The mandala provides a scheme by which human society and cosmic forces are coordinated within a single spatial system. Here, king and god share a common central location. The power of the presiding deity is manifested inside the mandala, and his protective influence emanates outward in all directions. The royal founder of the city activates this divine energy, since it is he who establishes the cosmic mandala of the ideal capital.

The cosmic dimensions of royal action are realized in other undertakings: for instance, the construction of a temple or sponsorship of festivities associated with the worship of a popular god or goddess. Well-defined rites articulate this component of royal authority, especially coronation ceremonies and other festivals that empower the royal figure, his weapons and army and, in the broadest sense, his entire realm. Since the Hindu king continually requires divine sanction, both within his capital and beyond, he lavishly supports Hindu deities and sometimes also non-Hindu beings. It is particularly important that divinities are accommodated within the royal city, which is in a sense the king's own household. The presence of gods and goddesses in the temples patronized by king and court demonstrates the sanctity of the royal domain.

For Vijayanagara to have functioned as an ideal Hindu capital it had to be a city of both kings and gods. This was achieved by the development of a royal center distinct from a sacred center. Though these two zones are spatially separated within the layout of Vijayanagara, they are conceptually linked. Since the king and the royal household were in daily contact with gods, palaces are situated close

(11) North entrance to the Ramachandra temple at core of the royal center, with processional friezes sculpted on the outer walls.

15

to shrines, and royal enclosures include temple complexes. Accordingly, a temple complex rather than a palace stands at the heart of Vijayanagara in the middle of the royal center. This shrine is dedicated to Rama, divine hero of the Ramayana epic.

Rama is a god of outstanding importance for the Vijayanagara rulers. As portrayed in the Ramayana, this hero embodied all the virtues of the ideal Hindu king, descending to earth to right all wrongs and destroy all evil. Rama ruled from the mythical city of Ayodhya, ideal of the perfect urban society where all men lived together in peace and harmony. The Vijayanagara kings compared themselves with Rama, and their historical records equate the king's realm, particularly his capital, with that of the god. "In the same city did Harihara dwell, as in former times Rama dwelt in the city Ayodhya" reads an inscription of one early ruler. This equation of terrestrial and epical worlds meant that the Vijayanagara king manifested the heroic and regal qualities of his divine counterpart and that his royal city housed the perfect Hindu society.

The importance of Rama for the Vijayanagara kings is demonstrated by the shrine dedicated to this god under the name Ramachandra, located at the most powerful point within the conceptual mandala of the city. More than any other building at Vijayanagara, the Ramachandra shrine symbolizes the meeting of kings and gods. This home of the god is linked spatially with the world of the ruler, since it is surrounded by palaces and other structures associated with the public and private activities of the court. The sculptures of royal elephants, horses, soldiers, and courtly women on the outside of the temple illustrate the king's world. In contrast, the carvings on the inside portray the world of the god by showing episodes from the Ramayana. The temple is coordinated with the landscape in which the city is set by being aligned with prominent sites identified with the Ramayana story.

Movement within the city is another means by which kings and gods meet at Vijayanagara. Ritual circular procession in a clockwise direction is an important act of homage to a Hindu deity or to a king, and such circular movement is incorporated into the layouts of Hindu temples and palaces. The system of roadways and alleys within the royal center at Vijayanagara permits a ritual circumambulation which proceeds from the private and public zones of the royal center to the Ramachandra shrine. Circumambulation is depicted pictorially in the carved reliefs of animals, soldiers, and women. These proceed in a clockwise direction around the temple walls, as do the panels of Ramayana episodes. All important roadways within the royal center converge on the Ramachandra temple, emphasizing the focal role of this monument.

(12) Columned porch and parapet with plaster figures in front of the main shrine of the Ramachandra temple.

CAPITAL AND EMPIRE

T he Deccan plateau, rising several hundred meters above sea level, is cut off from the Arabian Sea on the west and the Bay of Bengal on the east by forested slopes known as ghats. To the north lie the Vindhya hills that separate the Deccan from the river plains of northern India; other hills mark the beginning of a semitropical zone to the south. The Deccan is a dry territory traversed by great rivers such as the Godavari, Krishna, and Tungabhadra. Most settlements in the region are dependent on irrigation from wells and reservoirs. The characteristic Deccan landscape consists of flat or gently undulating plains with distant horizons. Such wide panoramas are occasionally interrupted by abrupt outcrops of red sandstone or of gray and pink granite. The absence of natural barriers means that frontiers between different kingdoms and chiefdoms were rarely fixed; on the contrary, they were frequently disputed. Indeed, up until the foundation of Vijayanagara, the Deccan was never under the control of a ruler who could unify it into a single state.

This was the situation in the last years of the thirteenth century, when the army of the Delhi sultan invaded southern India. With their superior military capability, especially their expert cavalry, the Muslim commanders easily swept away the Hindu kingdoms of the Deccan. The invasion was decisive: the Muslim army defeated the troops of the Hindu rulers and plundered the treasuries of palaces and temples. By the beginning of the fourteenth century, the Muslims had established themselves as the dominant military presence in the peninsula. Their principal headquarters were at Daulatabad in the northern Deccan and at Madurai, in the Tamil zone far to the south. But the Muslim occupation was not to last long; within a few decades, the Delhi sultan recalled his army to assist in wars elsewhere. The region was plunged into chaos once again.

After the Muslim retreat from southern India, several local chiefs who had survived the occupation reasserted their authority. Among these were the Sangama brothers, probably warriors in the service of Kampila who controlled a sparsely populated and relatively remote territory in the heart of the Deccan. This contained the fortified settlement of Anegondi on the north bank of the Tungabhadra River, and, about two kilometers to the southwest, the small sacred site of Hampi, overlooking the south bank of the river.

By the end of the first half of the fourteenth century, two of the Sangama brothers, Harihara and Bukka, had emerged as the most powerful Hindu leaders in the Dec-

(13) Elephant stables overlooking the parade ground in the royal center as viewed from the arcaded veranda of an adjacent structure.

an. Among their first acts was to worship at the Hampi shrines, where they sought the support of local divinities. Near this holy place they established their headquarters, naming it Vijayanagara, City of Victory. That their new capital was appropriately named became evident as the Sangama brothers extended their influence. Almost all of southern India was brought under their authority within merely a few decades; Muslim invaders were expelled and rival Hindu rulers subdued. The rapidly expanding Sangama territory, which soon assumed imperial proportions, was controlled from Vijayanagara. In time, it came to be known as the Vijayanagara empire.

The army of the Sangamas was the first in the Deccan to counter the Muslim forces, effectively checking the expansion of the sultans into the region. The remarkable political success of the Sangama brothers may be explained by the sheer numbers of their forces but also by their ability to embrace improved military techniques. The Sangamas imposed throughout their empire a system of tribute that made them wealthy. These revenues supported the formidable army of the Vijayanagara rulers and the spectacular growth of their capital.

The rule of the Sangama dynasty lasted almost a century and a half, and it was not until 1485 that they were usurped by another dynasty. During their long rule the Sangamas were often challenged by competing Hindu kings as well as by rebellious governors. They were also in continuous conflict with the Muslim rulers of the newly founded Bahmani kingdom to the north. The Sangama-Bahmani wars were mainly concerned with the control of the Raichur doab, a fertile zone that lay midway between Vijayanagara and Gulbarga, the Bahmani capital. Despite periodic strife, agreements were occasionally drawn up between Hindu and Muslim rulers, only to be broken again by fresh disagreements.

The first inscriptions of the Sangamas, the most reliable historical records of the time, refer to the god Virupaksha as the protective deity of the royal household. As a result of this sponsorship, the Virupaksha shrine at Hampi was developed into a major temple. This act of piety was an essential step in the transformation of these local chiefs into a royal dynasty with imperial claims. While the Sangamas made gifts to gods at shrines throughout the empire, they maintained their loyalty to Virupaksha at Hampi, the nucleus of Vijayanagara's sacred center. The early Vijayanagara kings were advised by Vidyaranya, religious leader of the prestigious Shaiva monastery at Sringeri in the wooded hills southwest of the capital.

The seat of the Vijayanagara rulers, the royal center established some two kilometers south of the Tungabhadra, served as the residence of kings, courtiers, and military officials. Here, too, was built a small Virupaksha shrine that duplicated the cult at Hampi. A recently discovered inscription mentions that one of the gateways in the encircling walls of the royal center led into the "city of Bukkaraya," that is, of Bukka I (ruled 1354/5–77). Thus, the fortifications protecting the royal center of the capital must already have been standing in the middle of the fourteenth century. It is likely that the multistoried platform erected upon the highest part of this zone also dates from these early years. The lively carvings that cover the lower stages of this platform illustrate ceremonial and hunting activities. This monument is linked by tradition with the Mahanavami, a festival developed by the Sangamas into a spectacular annual event.

Vijayanagara's fame attracted numerous visitors, including foreigners, some of whom published accounts of their visits. Among the memoirs from the Sangama period are those of the Italian visitor Nicolo di Conti in about 1420 and Abdul Razzaq, the emissary sent to India by the Muslim ruler of Herat in 1443, during the reign of Devaraya II (ruled 1424–46). Di Conti's overall impression of Vijayanagara was of a vast fortified citadel encompassing mountains and valleys. He noted the populous inhabitants of the capital and the splendor of the Mahanavami festival. Abdul Razzaq prefaced his report of the city with a confession that its "inhabitants have no equals in the world." Only after passing through seven concentric fortifications did this visitor arrive at the innermost palace of the king, where he observed an audience hall, a hall of justice, a hall of the chief minister, and a mint. He noted the elephant stables with separate compartments for each animal and the bazaars arranged in long, colonnaded streets. Abdul Razzaq's chronicle ends with a description of the great civic festival, during which the visitor was presented to the king, who was seated on a golden throne studded with precious gems.

Abdul Razzaq's account is of significance since it was used by early archaeologists at Vijayanagara to label monuments of the royal center and to designate parts of this zone as the king's palace enclosure, the enclosure of the chief minister, and the mint. Unfortunately, Abdul Razzaq provided insufficient details of buildings and their locations for such identifications to be accepted with certainty. A century and a half of subsequent modifications also changed the forms and uses of monuments. These designations have not been adopted here.

The visit of Abdul Razzaq coincided with a period of major construction at the capital, which greatly enhanced its splendor. By the mid-fifteenth century, during the reign of Devaraya II, an ellipse of fortifications more than four kilometers across contained the royal center. In the middle stood the Ramachandra temple, a hundred-columned hall, and numerous other civic buildings, including

Above: (14) Dilapidated shrines and halls facing onto the road that runs northeastward from the Ramachandra temple.

Below: (15) Enclosure walls of the royal center, with ruined structure in the corner.

Temple Lamps

Opposite the principal gate stand four columns, two gilded and the other two copper, from which, owing to their great age as it seems to me, the gold has worn off. That which stands nearest the gate of the temple was given by this King Crisnarao [Krishnadevaraya] who now reigns here, and the others by his predecessors. As soon as you enter this idol-shrine, you perceive from pillar to pillar . . . many little holes in which stand oil lamps, which burn, so they tell me, every night, and they will be in number two thousand five hundred or three thousand lights.

DOMINGO PAES, Portuguese visitor to Vijayanagara, 1520-22

Opposite: (16) Monolithic lamp column at the end of the Hampi bazaar lighting the chariot street.

Above: (17) Collapsing Madhava temple overlooked by the octagonal watchtower in the royal center; elephant stables are in the distance.

Below: (18) Interior columns of the Ramachandra temple, the shafts covered with sculptures of the god Vishnu.

the Mahanavami platform already referred to. Palaces and small shrines must have surrounded these monuments, some of which are now being revealed by clearing and excavation.

The last two decades of the fifteenth century and the first decade of the sixteenth were marked at Vijayanagara by successive military coups by the Saluva and Tuluva families. A similarly turbulent situation prevailed in the Muslim territories to the north, where the Bahmani state fragmented into the smaller kingdoms of Bijapur, Bidar, Golconda, and Ahmadnagar. Furthermore, by the end of the fifteenth century the Portuguese had arrived on the western coast of the Deccan, where, from their principal port at Goa, they gained control of the Arabian sea trade. The involvement of the Portuguese in the affairs of both Vijayanagara and the Deccan Muslim states introduced further conflict and intrigue.

Political stability at Vijayanagara was restored under the Tuluva dynasty, the greatest rulers of which were Krishnadevaraya (ruled 1510–29) and his stepbrother Achyutadevaraya (ruled 1529–42). During the first half of the sixteenth century Vijayanagara enjoyed a sustained period of internal peace and prosperity. The era was marked by an artistic and cultural efflorescence, with the erection of large-scale temples under the sponsorship of the royal family and other prominent individuals. Both Krishnadevaraya and Achyutadevaraya were successful in most of their military campaigns against their Hindu and Muslim rivals; they toured extensively in southern India, inspecting fortified outposts and making donations to deities at different religious sites. In particular, these kings increased the patronage of the god Venkateshvara, whose sanctuary at Tirumala was located some 400 kilometers southeast of the capital.

At Vijayanagara the reigns of these two emperors, as well as that of their successor, Sadashiva, who ascended the throne in 1542, were marked by much building. The sacred center on the south bank of the Tungabhadra was developed by extending the older Virupaksha shrine and by founding entirely new complexes dedicated to Krishna, Tiruvengalanatha, and Vithala, all aspects of Vishnu. Large temples were also erected near the outlying settlements that constituted the suburban centers of the capital. During the reign of Sadashiva, power was increasingly appropriated by the military commander Ramaraya, father-in-law of Krishnadevaraya. By the middle of the sixteenth century the empire was virtually controlled by him. This situation, however, did not affect temple patronage, for Ramaraya was an ardent sponsor of Vaishnava shrines, many of which were expanded on a grand scale.

New suburban centers at Vijayanagara were laid out in

(19) Quarters of the royal elephants used by the king in ceremony and war; each elephant was assigned its own chamber.

the first half of the sixteenth century. According to the Portuguese visitor Domingo Paes, who was at the capital from about 1520 to 1522, Krishnadevaraya himself resided in a royal settlement some distance to the southwest. The only surviving evidence of this and other peripheral settlements are isolated temples, tombs, gateways, reservoirs, and fragmentary fortification walls. However, ruins of ceremonial and courtly structures dating from the Tuluva period still survive in the royal center of the capital. The density of archaeological features in this zone, together with the profusion of additions and alterations, indicates that rebuilding continued until the abandonment of the site. Significantly, only a few temples of any importance were erected in the royal center under the Tuluvas, though older ceremonial structures, such as the Mahanavami platform, were substantially renovated. It would seem that this zone continued to serve as a site of civic ceremony throughout the first half of the sixteenth century, even when other districts of the capital were preferred for royal residences.

Important descriptions of Vijayanagara under the Tuluvas are provided by Domingo Paes and by another Portuguese, Fernao Nuniz, who was at the capital during the reign of Achyutadevaraya. Paes observed the city's stone walls, which ran over the rocky hills, and the many gates with towers. He was unable to estimate the size of Vijayanagara's population "because it cannot all be seen from any one spot." He acknowledged that "the people in this city are countless in number, so much so that I do not wish to write it down for fear it should be thought fabulous." He continued: "What I saw . . . seemed as large as large as Rome, and very beautiful to the sight; there are many groves of tree within it . . . many orchards and gardens with fruit trees . . . many conduits of water which flow in the midst of it, and in places there are lakes." He concluded that Vijayanagara is "the best provided city in the world."

Paes was received by Krishnadevaraya in his new royal residence, "a league" away from Vijayanagara. The visitor described the old palace, presumably in the royal center, listing the heavily guarded gates, the many inner courtyards with painted walls, an underground chamber, a bedchamber, another room completely paneled in ivory, a treasury, a room with a "cot" suspended from chains of gold, and a dance hall ornamented with carved animals and figures. Most of these palace buildings had columns of carved stone or wood, with flat roofs above. Paes witnessed the daily routine of the king, who met with his ministers and other officials in a "building made in the shape of a porch," which served as the council chamber. Within the city the bazaars and their wares attracted this visitor's attention, as did the gilded columns and towers of the temples. Like Abdul Razzaq some eighty years earlier,

Paes was invited to attend the Mahanavami celebrations, which he described at some length.

The empire experienced increasing difficulties toward the middle of the sixteenth century, due partly to a deterioration of Vijayanagara's internal political ties and to a worsening of relations with the sultans to the north. Sadashiva was never permitted to assert his royal authority, and the young king was eventually imprisoned by his uncle, the regent Ramaraya.

Ramaraya had been particularly arrogant in his dealings with the Deccan sultans. Since no single Muslim ruler could hope to defeat the superior Vijayanagara forces, the regent had little reason to feel insecure. Only when the Bijapur sultan took unprecedented initiative in proposing an alliance of all of the Muslim armies did Ramaraya make preparations for war.

On January 26, 1565, both forces faced each other across a battlefield some one hundred kilometers northwest of the Hindu capital. The results were swift and catastrophic for Vijayanagara. Ramaraya was killed almost immediately, and his decapitated head was raised high on a stake. At the sight of this trophy, the Vijayanagara army took flight. Several officers possibly defected to the other side, facilitating the Muslim victory. Led by Ramaraya's brother Tirumala, the Vijayanagara forces retreated to the capital, released the imprisoned king, and collected the imperial treasury and throne. They then fled to the fort of Penukonda, two hundred kilometers to the southeast, leaving the capital without any defence against the Muslim forces.

There is no reliable eyewitness account of the sack of Vijayanagara, but the ruined buildings which remain speak clearly of the devastation. Fires were set in temples and gateways and stone blocks broken to pieces; judging from empty sanctuaries and wall niches, sculptures were smashed or simply removed. Timber superstructures of palaces were burned, and only charred fragments have been discovered in the excavations. Precious materials and objects were plundered by the attackers; what remained was eventually removed by generations of treasure seekers.

Yet, tellingly, not all of Vijayanagara's buildings were vandalized. Most of the shrines dedicated to the god Shiva escaped destruction altogether. This was in marked contrast to sanctuaries dedicated to other Hindu deities, which were irreparably damaged. The relatively complete condition of the Virupaksha complex at Hampi, for example, has suggested to some historians that there was some agreement ensuring the temple's preservation between the Vijayanagara commanders who worshiped this god and the Muslim leaders. Nor were all the courtly structures willfully damaged; their present dilapidated condition is due mostly to decay.

It is also possible that some of the Vijayanagara monuments were erected, or at least repaired, after the sack of the capital. Tirumala occupied the city for a time after the Muslim forces had departed, in an attempt to repopulate the site. Cesare Federici, an Italian visitor to Vijayanagara in 1567, described Tirumala's palace, with its sequence of courts and soldiers guarding the gates. Though Tirumala attempted to regain control of the empire, Sadashiva remained the titular head. But this obstacle was removed when the king was murdered in 1570. Tirumala then proclaimed himself emperor, founding the fourth and last Vijayanagara dynasty of Aravidu kings.

The proximity of Vijayanagara to the Muslim territories to the north compelled Tirumala to move his permanent headquarters back to Penukonda. Two of his inscriptions dated 1568 mention that Vijayanagara was destroyed and in ruins. But the Muslims must periodically have occupied the city, since another Italian traveler, Filippo Sassetti, met a governor from Bijapur there in 1585. But by the time that Ferishta was composing his Persian-language history of the Deccan in the first decade of the seventeenth century, Vijayanagara was an abandoned ruin.

For the more than two hundred years preceding its destruction, Vijayanagara was the seat of a ruling dynasty, and its destiny was inextricably bound up with that of the imperial household. No city existed at the site before the foundation of the capital, nor did the capital survive the catastrophe of 1565. The economic and cultural life of Vijayanagara was entirely determined by the fortunes of the king, the dominant patron and consumer. Many of the largest building projects within the capital were commissioned by the ruler, who was also responsible for urban ceremonies and festivals.

The Vijayanagara kings believed that their actions were in harmony with traditional Hindu models of kingship, such as those specified in the chapters on polity contained in the shastras. These treatises explain the combination of political, moral, and cosmic ideals the Hindu monarch was expected to fulfill. Inscriptions on monuments at the capital, as well as on copperplates found throughout the empire, provide information on the mundane matters of dynastic history, economic affairs, and local agricultural conditions. But these inscriptions are also moral and cosmological statements, since they liken the brilliance of the ruler to that of the gods and claim divine origin for the royal family. Literary works of the period, too, including histories of particular Vijayanagara rulers, outline the diverse activities of the ideal Hindu monarch. The king was the upholder of traditional law, moral well-being, and material prosperity. He defended society through war, conquest, and plunder. The annual cycle of the Vijayanagara king's life was divided in two. During the monsoon season, ruler, court, and army resided at Vijayanagara; during the remainder of the year they traveled in vast retinues through-

out the empire and beyond on missions of pilgrimage and war. Significantly, the moment of transition from the passive to active periods of the year was marked at Vijayanagara by the celebration of the Mahanavami festival.
hanavami festival.

As the representative of traditional law, or dharma, the Vijayanagara king was expected to preserve the accepted divisions of society. Accordingly, he was frequently known as "defender of dharma and protector of caste." Arbitrating disputes was one means by which the Vijayanagara monarch maintained order, and the royal person was himself the highest court of appeal. No bureaucratic institution "made" law, but officers of the king presumably carried out his decisions. The ruler sought the advice of a royal council on important matters, such as imperial revenues, the strength of the army, and the making of war. The council was composed of ministers, including commander of the armed forces and overseer of the royal household. The ministers's power sometimes threatened that of the king. As previously noted, there were two successful military coups at Vijayanagara.

Excavations in the largest enclosures of the royal center at Vijayanagara have provided substantial information about the king's public life. One platform with one hundred stone footings, once a square hall with large timber columns, may have served as a hall of audience and a place where the king and his council adjudicated disputes. Immediately to the south are the remains of other square and rectangular halls with open, columned interiors. The precise purposes of these buildings are unknown, but it is likely that they were connected with the public activities of the king and those in his service.

Because of constant risk of invasion, usurpation, and assassination, the king had to be concerned about his personal safety. The formidable military force concentrated at Vijayanagara was composed of infantry, cavalry, elephants, and, in later years, artillery. Fernao Nuniz estimated that Krishnadevaraya had a permanent army of fifty thousand soldiers, with six thousand horsemen comprising the palace guard. Two hundred of these troops were with the king everywhere he went. Also in royal service were twenty thousand spearmen and shield-bearers, three thousand men to look after the elephants, sixteen hundred grooms to attend the horses, three hundred horse trainers, and no fewer than two thousand artisans. These figures may be exaggerated, yet the army was by far the greatest expense for the Vijayanagara king, since soldiers received cash from the imperial treasury. Nuniz also notes that the king spent considerably for the purchase of horses, which had to be imported from Arabia and paid for in gold. These animals were transported to Vijayanagara first by Arab traders and in later years by Portuguese merchants. During the reign of Achyutadevaraya, according to Nuniz,

no fewer than 13,000 horses arrived each year at Vijayanagara. Firearms, in general use from the fifteenth century onward, were another major expense.

Several monuments in the royal center of Vijayanagara can be linked with military activities. Among the best-preserved are the stables which housed the royal elephants used by the king in both peace and war. The long, imposing stables, roofed by domes and vaults, face on a spacious open area which may have been used for military displays. A second building opening onto the same area may have functioned as a reviewing stand or as a setting for mock battles and wrestling matches. Another nearby building, distinguished by its gabled roof, could have served either as a store for precious items such as weapons and gunpowder or as an exercise hall. The archaeologists now working in the royal center have suggested that several structures excavated within the largest enclosure in this zone were intended as accommodation for the king's private guard.

The military machinery of Vijayanagara was supplemented by a system of espionage directed by royal officers. The king received daily reports regarding everything that took place in the capital and throughout the empire, and he met regularly with subordinate chiefs and governors. Among the structures connected with the network of royal surveillance are gateways and watchtowers. These were strategically located on all major roadways and controlled access to the king's zone. Watchtowers rising above the enclosure walls guarded the approaches from different directions.

The daily life of the king was highly ritualized and included numerous audiences, receptions, and ceremonies. Krishnadevaraya's personal routine, as observed by Domingo Paes, gives a good idea of these activities. The monarch rose before daybreak, was massaged with oil, and then performed vigorous exercises, including wrestling. After being washed by a brahmin, he performed worship at a palace shrine. The king then gave audience to "those who bore office throughout the empire, and who governed the different cities." He received the chiefs and governors, who saluted the royal presence by raising their joined palms above their heads but who did not directly address him. On such occasions, the king listened to petitions and bestowed favors and gifts. Throughout these audiences the king sat on a mat or reclined against a cushion. He was surrounded by a retinue of officers, servants, and guards who constituted his personal staff and who displayed umbrellas, banners, standards, fly whisks, and other royal emblems.

Among the structures that may have been linked with these kingly activities within the royal center are the hun-

(20) Two-storied pavilion in the royal center, known as the Lotus Mahal, possibly a reception hall of the king.

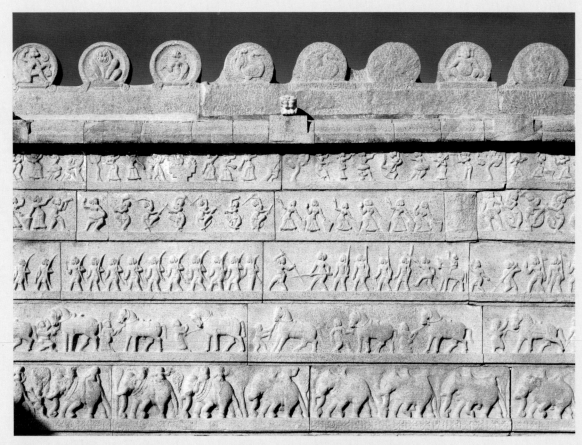

(21) Festival processions carved on the outer walls of the Ramachandra temple.

MAHANAVAMI FESTIVAL

As soon as the king is seated, the captains who waited without making their entrance approach and make their salaams to the king, and then take their places in the pavilions. As soon as these nobles have finished entering, the captains of the troops approach with shields and spears, and afterwards the captains of the archers; these officers are all stationed on the ground around the arena in front of the elephants, and they constitute the king's guard. As soon as the soldiers have all taken their places the women begin to dance, while some of them place themselves in the circular galleries at their gate of entrance.

Then the wrestlers begin their play. There are blows so severe as to break teeth, and put out eyes, and disfigure faces, so much so that here and there men are carried off speechless. They have their captains and judges, who are there to put each on an equal footing in the field, and also to adjust the honors to him who wins.

As soon as ever the sun is down many torches are lit and some great flambeaux made of cloth; and these are placed in the arena in such a way that the whole is as light as day, and even along the top of the walls for on all the battlements are lighted lamps, and the place where the king sits is all full of torches. As soon as these are lit up there are introduced many very graceful plays and contrivances. There enter battles of people on horseback; others come with casting-nets, fishing and capturing men that are in the arena. When these amusements are ended, they begin to throw up many rockets and many different sorts of fires, also castles that burn and fling out from themselves many bombs and rockets.

When these fireworks are finished, there enter many horses covered with trappings and cloths of very fine stuff of the king's colors, and with many roses and flowers on their heads and necks, and with their bridles all gilded; in front of these horses goes a horse with two state-umbrellas of the king. In front of this horse goes another caracoling and prancing, as do all horses here, being trained in that art. These horses, then, pass twice around the arena and place themselves in the middle of the area in five or six lines, one before the other, and the king's horse in front of them, all facing the king.

As soon as they are arranged in this way you will see issuing from inside twenty-five or thirty female-doorkeepers, with canes in their hands and whips on their shoulders; and then close to these come many eunuchs, and after these eunuchs come many women playing many trumpets and drums and pipes and viols, and behind these women will come some twenty women-porters, with canes in their hands all covered with silver, and close to them come women clothed in the following manner. They have very rich and fine silk cloths; on the head they wear high caps, and on these caps they wear flowers made of large pearls; collars on the neck with jewels of gold very richly set with many emeralds and diamonds and rubies and pearls; and beside this many strings of pearls; on the waist many girdles of gold and precious stones. They carry in their hands vessels of gold each as large as a small cask of water; inside these are some loops made of pearls, and inside all this a lighted lamp. They come in regular order one before the other, in all perhaps sixty women fair and young, from sixteen to twenty years of age. So great is the weight of the bracelets and gold and jewels carried by them that many of them cannot support them, and women accompany them assisting them by supporting their arms. In this manner and in this array they proceed three times round the horses, and at the end retire into the palace.

When these women retire the horses also go, and then come the elephants, and after making their salaams they too retire. As soon as they are gone, the king retires by a small door.

DOMINGO PAES, Portuguese visitor to Vijayanagara, 1520-22

31

dred-columned hall already mentioned and multidomed and vaulted pavilions built in a distinctly Islamic-influenced style. These courtly buildings have spacious interiors within which the king may have been seated in the presence of subordinates. Open halls with regularly spaced columns were also capable of accommodating large groups of people.

Within the palace the king enjoyed various entertainments, such as wrestling, dance, and music. While the women of the royal household were isolated behind protective walls, the monarch was attended by beautiful courtesans who lived in the city. Their attractions and accomplishments seem also to have been much appreciated by the Persian and European visitors, judging from the accounts of Abudul Razzaq and Domingo Paes. These courtesans enjoyed royal privileges and were permitted to visit the king and his wives. They were often highly educated and cultured and were celebrated for diverting the king's gaze, even though they were not generally permitted to live within the royal precinct.

Among the courtly monuments are bathing pavilions and halls for performances of music and drama. Varied and elaborately decorated architectural forms characterize these courtly structures, many of which still stand relatively complete. Outside the city, in the nearby forested hills, sporting expeditions were organized to hunt deer, boar, and sometimes wild elephants. The king was accompanied by women of the court during leisurely picnics. On these occasions, the royal entourage spent afternoons and evenings in the orchards and wooded groves.

The king's private household attracted the curiosity of foreign visitors, all of whom commented on the great beauty and wealth of the Vijayanagara court women. They also noted the diverse ethnic origins of the women, which reflected the territorial claims of the king's domain. Domingo Paes speculated that Krishnadevaraya enjoyed the pleasures of three to four hundred wives and altogether employed about twelve hundred women as dancers, singers, musicians, and astrologers. Each of the important wives had her own female attendants and servants, generally guarded by eunuchs. No man was allowed to enter the women's apartments unless specially permitted by the king. He did not live with his female entourage but would visit his favorite consort in the secluded women's apartments. These formed an important, though separate, part of the royal center. Enclosures with high walls contained palaces surrounded by subsidiary buildings. The palaces were approached through complex entryways with numerous doorways and checkpoints. Such palaces appear to have been primarily used as residences, with associated cooking and bathing facilities. Other structures nearby may have been for reception and entertainment.

Certainly the most spectacular royal occasion at Vijayanagara was the Mahanavami festival. This took place after the monsoon, at the beginning of the dry winter season. As a religious ceremony, the Mahanavami commemorated the day on which Rama propitiated the powerful goddess Durga before marching against the evil Ravana. It also marked the triumph of Durga over the buffalo demon Mahisha. As a political event, however, the Mahanavami was a celebration of anticipated victory, the principal rite being the infusion of the royal throne and weapons with cosmic energy. Paes, who left the most detailed account of the festival, noted a "house of victory" containing the shrine at which the king worshiped and in front of which animals were sacrificed. The king was seated on a nearby throne, where he received the chiefs and governors of the empire. For nine days there were magnificent processions of elephants, horses, armed soldiers, women, and servants. Performances of music and dance, mock battles, and wrestling matches also took place. The nights were devoted to feasting and to fireworks displays. On the tenth day the king reviewed the troops assembled on the plains outside the city.

The Mahanavami was the one annual occasion at Vijayanagara when the chiefs, governors, and lesser officials of the empire were compelled to gather at the capital. Their presence at Vijayanagara affirmed their willingness to support the king throughout the coming year. The honors that the ruler bestowed at this time affirmed the hierarchy of status among his subordinates, all of whom had publicly to acknowledge his supremacy. Not least, the Mahanavami was the beginning of the new financial year. Domingo Paes notes that all taxes due to the Vijayanagara king had to be settled at this time. The ruler resumed his more public and aggressive activities after these rites, for the Mahanavami marked the beginning of the appropriate season for pilgrimage and war. As head and protector of the empire, the Vijayanagara ruler proceeded to travel throughout his realm, distributing wealth, participating in religious rites, and adjudicating disputes.

The great multistoried stone platform in the royal center at Vijayanagara is traditionally identified with the Mahanavami and partly corresponds to Paes's "house of victory." The lowest two stages of this monument platform are covered with reliefs illustrating scenes of reception, hunting, wrestling matches, and processions of horses, elephants, and female dancers and musicians. Another possible depiction of the Mahanavami appears on the outer face of the enclosure walls of the nearby Ramachandra temple. Here are carved parades of elephants and horses, armed troops in different formations, and female dancers and musicians. Royal figures are also included, either seated on thrones or mounted on horses, with parasols held above their heads by attendants.

Above: (22) Multistoried platform, with steps in the middle of one side, used during the Mahanavami festival; bathing tank is in front.

Below: (23) Musicians, royal horses with bearded attendants, and hunting scenes on the sides of the platform.

THE IMPREGNABLE FORTRESS

Vijayanagara's dramatic landscape creates a vast natural fortress for the city, the rugged hills north of the Tungabhadra having afforded protection from both Muslim and Hindu invaders. The river, almost impassable on the north and west, also served as a barrier. That the Hindu capital survived for more than two hundred years on the edge of territory heatedly disputed with the sultans is a measure of the city's strength. Despite the fact that Vijayanagara was besieged on a number of occasions, it was never taken by force. Only after the disastrous battle of 1565, when the city lay undefended, was it sacked and burned.

Hemakuta's fortifications, overlooking Hampi from the south, may date from the period of the first Vijayanagara kings. The hill is surrounded by strong walls, with double-storied gateways surveying the Tungabhadra valley. It is unlikely, however, that the Vijayanagara kings ever resided on Hemakuta, since by the middle of the fourteenth century the royal center had already been laid out. This zone was once surrounded by a ring of fortifications with gateways on all sides. The walls and gateways stand ruined and isolated. But the royal center was only the nucleus of a much larger zone, the urban core, which was also protected by a circuit of massive fortifications. Almost all of the walls of the urban core still stand, in some places to a height of more than six meters. Their outer faces are constructed of gigantic blocks of granite fitted together without mortar; earth packed with rubble fills their interiors. Square and rectangular bastions are positioned at regular intervals. Lookout posts on top of these bastions guard the approaches to the city.

The fortifications of Vijayanagara's urban core define an approximately oval-shaped area more than four kilometers along its southwest-northeast axis. The irregular configuration of the walls is partly explained by the rugged topography, which was ingeniously exploited to defend the city. Wherever feasible, the fortifications follow the rocky ridges, taking advantage of the natural defenses of the site. This is particularly true on the north and east sides of the urban core, where walls scramble up and over the boulders. The fortifications also traverse the valleys between ridges, generally following the shortest possible routes. They are more linear on the south and west sides of the urban core, where the landscape opens up.

The royal center and urban core, one within the other, each with its own ring of walls, were only the inner forts of Vijayanagara. The descriptions of foreign visitors suggest that there was an even more extensive system of concentric protective fortifications. Abdul Razzaq notes that

(24) Entry to the urban core of the city through Bhima's gateway, protected by formidable barbican walls.

35

he had to pass through seven "forts" in order to reach the king's palace. If, indeed, seven walls existed, not all are now visible. There are, however, substantial remains of a third concentric ring beyond the urban core, portions of which are evident southeast of the site, where walls serve as a dam for a large reservoir. The outer defenses consisted of earthen ramparts and lines of closely spaced boulders, only scant traces of which are preserved.

Vijayanagara's fortifications are interrupted by substantial gateways that provided the city with security. These structures—checkpoints for people, animals, and goods— were where duties were paid. Gateways had central passageways closed off by heavy wooden doors at night or during siege. These doors were all burned during the sack of the city, but an idea of their form may be had from a stone imitation of a typical door; this lies on the ground near the Mahanavami platform in the royal center. The inner passageways of gateways are flanked by colonnades raised on masonry platforms, with horizontal beams supporting upper chambers. The most elaborate example of this scheme is Bhima's gateway within the urban core. This has triple sets of carved corbels carrying the roof slabs. The outer gateway on the northeast road of the urban core still has portions of its upper chamber. The walls have Islamic-style, pointed arches and an ornamental parapet.

Gateways were defended by barbicans, which created outer enclosures with high, stone-faced walls. The entrances to these enclosures are generally unaligned with the gateways, making it necessary to take one or more turns before passing through. Shrines within these enclosures are dedicated to Hanuman, the popular monkey god celebrated for his strength and courage, or to Ganesha, the elephant-headed god who protected travelers. Images of armed doorkeepers or heroes such as Bhima are sculpted on doorjambs and wall blocks. The entrances to enclosures are generally plain. An exception is the large dome supported on four broad arches that rises above the entrance to the outer gateway on the southeast road of the urban core.

Though the buildings in the middle of the royal center were less strongly defended, the surrounding walls and gateways afforded protection and privacy. The royal center consists of a number of irregular enclosures, each defined by high, tapering walls. The strongest of these walls have interlocking stone blocks with tightly fitted joints that create ingenious patterns. Some walls are layers of packed earth originally covered with plaster. Communication and movement between the different enclosures of the royal center were controlled by large gateway structures. Only the stone-clad foundations and stone column blocks of these structures survive, their upper timber and stone rubble portions having long ago disappeared. The remains of doorways, courts, and connecting passageways occupy a large proportion of the space within the royal enclosures. Evidently, considerable care was taken to restrict access to the private apartments of the king and his household.

Gateways within the royal center and in the surrounding outer circuits of walls indicate where roads entered the capital. Worn pavement slabs, ramps, and steps are also sometimes visible. Where roads are buried under accumulated earth or have eroded away, their routes are suggested by the alignments of temples, shrines, columned structures, monolithic lamp columns, and wells.

Many of Vijayanagara's important roads lead into the royal center; others proceed around it, linking the outlying settlements of the city with the sacred center at Hampi. The most striking feature of this system is the convergence of roads on the royal center, in particular on the Ramachandra temple, the hub of movement within the urban core. But the roads leading to the sacred center are also of importance, since these are the routes still taken by pilgrims who come to bathe in the Tungabhadra before worshiping at the nearby Virupaksha temple.

Vijayanagara depended upon a regular supply of water, which, in the dry Deccan climate, was mostly provided by the summer monsoon and by sporadic winter rains. But the Vijayanagara kings also promoted large-scale irrigation projects to exploit the natural features of their valley. Small dams diverted water from the Tungabhadra into channels that irrigated fields at a considerable distance from the river. Great and small reservoirs, known as tanks, were created with earthen dam walls to trap rainwater; channels conducted water from large tanks across the Vijayanagara site. The hydraulic scheme that irrigates the valley today reuses portions of this original system. Many of the currently used water channels and dams actually belong to the Vijayanagara era.

The suburban settlements of the capital were associated with sizable tanks such as the large dams near the villages of Kamalapuram, southeast of the urban core, and Malpannagudi, further away to the southwest. Domingo Paes observed the construction of a massive reservoir outside Krishnadevaraya's new royal suburb. He saw sixty workmen being sacrificed after the dam failed several times. All that remains of this doomed project is a vast earthen wall bridging a valley on the outskirts of Hospet.

Another massive wall, now broken, runs across a small valley southeast of the royal center to create what must have been the largest reservoir within the urban core. The remains of another dam extend across the valley between the urban core and the sacred center south of Matanga Hill. The absence of structures or broken pottery in the vicinity of this dam, together with a brief inscription men-

Above: (26) Gateway leading to the river crossing to Anegondi at the boundary of the urban core, with part of the upper chamber still preserved.

Below: (27) Square watchtower appearing through the broken enclosure walls of the royal center.

Opposite: (28) Steps from an early Shiva temple lead down to water trapped in a rocky crevice on Hemakuta Hill.

City Walls and Gates

Returning, then, to the first gate of the city, before you arrive at it you pass a little piece of water and then you arrive at the wall, which is very strong, all of stonework, and it makes a bend before you arrive at the gate; and at the entrance of this gate are two towers, one on each side, which makes it very strong. It is large and beautiful. As soon as you pass inside there are two little temples.

DOMINGO PAES, Portuguese visitor to Vijayanagara, 1520-22

tioning a tank, suggests the original agricultural function of this part of the city. Today, irrigation supports a rich crop of banana trees and sugarcane. Elsewhere, especially along the roads, wells were dug into the ground, with flights of steps leading down to the water.

Remains of a complex hydraulic system are preserved in the royal center of the capital; here there are plaster-lined stone channels, drains, and aqueducts. Fresh water was collected in storage tanks, which ranged from deep wells and small square ponds to large, rectangular baths sealed with bricks and mortar. Waste water escaped through drains into sumps. Among the baths revealed in the recent excavations of the royal enclosures is a large, square tank with steps on four sides, entirely built with gray-green chlorite brought from distant quarries.

While some of these baths may have been connected with royal rituals, others were undoubtedly associated with courtly pleasure and entertainment. A large palace complex east of the enclosures in the royal center has an octagonal bath with an open colonnade around a central basin and a small platform in the middle. The series of linked water structures extending along the south side of the enclosures includes a square pavilion with a central water basin. Further west, an octagonal pavilion standing beside one of the roads once served as a small fountain.

The large and diverse population of Vijayanagara depended, in addition to water, on a regular supply of food and materials. Residents of the city and its suburbs had to be fed, clothed, housed, and provided in varying degrees with essential goods and luxuries. In addition to royal elephants and horses, domestic dray animals had to be maintained. While the means by which the city was provisioned is not yet understood in detail, foreign visitors all agree on the abundance of goods available in the city's markets. Abdul Razzaq notes the many irrigated gardens outside the urban core, while Domingo Paes comments on the trees shading the streets leading into the capital. The latter also mentions water channels and lakes, groves of palms, and orchards of fruit trees.

The visitors were delighted by crowded bazaars stocked with a large variety of merchandise. While some streets appear to have been occupied primarily by the houses of the rich and powerful, others were lined with the shops of merchants and craftsmen. Fernao Nuniz estimates that some two thousand beasts of burden entered the city with merchandise. Often, the streets of the city were so crowded with laden oxen that it was impossible to pass. In some streets fairs were held once a week. Markets offered grains and seeds such as rice, wheat, beans, and pulses. Almost no fresh vegetables are mentioned, but presumably these were numerous and varied, as were fruits such as

(29) Ruined temple beside the canal and road running along the south side of the irrigated valley.

MARKETS AND MERCHANTS

On every Friday you have a fair there, with many pigs and fowls and dried fish from the sea, and other things the produce of the country, of which I do not know the name; and in like manner a fair is held every day in different parts of the city. At the end of this street is the Moorish quarter, which is at the very end of the city, and of these Moors there are many who are natives of the country, and who are paid by the king and belong to his guard. In this city you will find men belonging to every nation and people, because of the great trade which it has, and the many precious stones there, principally diamonds.

This is the best provided city in the world, and is stocked with provisions, such as rice, wheat, grains, Indian-corn, and a certain amount of barley and beans, pulses, horse-gram, and many other seeds which grow in this country which are the food of the people. The streets and markets are full of laden oxen without count, so that you cannot get along for them, and in many streets you come upon so many of them that you have to wait for them to pass, or else have to go by another way. There is much poultry, and all kinds of wild fowl, and other birds which live in the lakes and which look like geese. All these birds and game animals they sell alive, and they are very cheap.

Then the sheep that they kill every day are countless, one could not number them, for in every street there are men who will sell you mutton. Then you see the many loads of limes that come each day, and also loads of sweet and sour oranges, and wild brinjals, and other garden stuff in such abundance as to stupefy one. For the state of this city is not like that of other cities, which often fail of supplies and provisions, for in this one everything abounds; and also the quantity of butter and oil and milk sold every day, that is athing I cannot refrain from mentioning; and as for the rearing of cows and buffaloes which goes on in this city, there is so much that you will go very far before you find another like it.

DOMINGO PAES, Portuguese visitor
to Vijayanagara, 1520-22

mangoes, oranges, limes, grapes, and pomegranates. Abdul Razzaq comments on the abundance of scented flowers in the markets. Oil, butter, and milk were also easily available. Many kinds of wild and domestic fowl were sold, and there were large quantities of meat. Sheep and goats were sacrificed each day at certain temples and then offered for sale together with pigs. Dried fish from the ocean and fresh fish from the Tungabhadra were displayed in the markets. River fish were caught with the aid of circular coracles made of cane covered with leather. (Similar boats are used today by fishermen on the Tungabhadra.) Live animals such as goats, sheep, cows, buffaloes, and horses were also available.

While foreign visitors noted the presence of durable goods such as wood and cloth, they were particularly impressed by the quantities of precious stones in certain markets. Paes observed rubies, diamonds, emeralds, and pearls. Of these, the diamonds were considered particularly valuable, Vijayanagara's mines being the largest in India at this time. No doubt many of these precious stones found their way into the jewelry worn by members of the court and into the regalia of temple images.

Several visitors provide descriptions of the actual market structures. Abdul Razzaq comments on a long and broad structure with an arch raised above. An inscription on a Jain temple on the northeast road of Vijayanagara's royal center identifies the road as the bazaar of the pan sellers. Pan is a mixture of areca nut, lime, and other ingredients wrapped in a betel leaf and chewed. A mild narcotic, it is taken widely and is offered to honored guests. Accordingly, Abdul Razzaq was offered pan during his interview with Devaraya II, and he gives an appreciative account of its ingredients and pleasurable effects.

Of the many and various specialists who must have produced and sold food and manufactured goods, foreign visitors give little information. Certainly, the capital included artisans such as potters, metalworkers, hide workers, and masons as well as fishermen, butchers, and jewelers. Where they lived and worked is as yet unknown. Paes suggests that some merchants and craftsmen were organized into guilds attached to temples in the city.

Archaeological reconnaissance in the region beyond Vijayanagara's urban core reveals the remains of fields and irrigation systems as well as of settlements with workshops where various goods were produced. The population of the greater Vijayanagara area was certainly larger than that of the present day and differently distributed. Outlying settlements surrounded by fields and tanks, now abandoned, were once linked to the city by roads. According to visitors' accounts, irrigation systems were greatly expanded in the early sixteenth century, particularly in the region of Hospet but also beyond the hills that form the eastern boundary of the fortified suburban area.

The foreign travelers comment on the various social groups of Vijayanagara's population. According to Paes, "In this city you will find men belonging to every nation and people, because of the great trade. . . ." The spectrum of linguistic, religious, ethnic, and professional communities found throughout the empire must have been represented at the capital. It is likely that these distinctive social groups were located in different areas of the city. While a cluster of Jain temples in the valley east of the royal center may indicate that followers of that cult resided nearby, the locations of most other groups are unknown.

Muslims have left the clearest record of their presence at Vijayanagara. Despite continuous strife between the Hindu kings and the sultans of the Muslim kingdoms to the north, there were regular exchanges of peoples, goods, artistic traditions, and, most important, military techniques. Muslim officers, with their valuable experience of horses and firearms, were recruited to serve in the army of the Vijayanagara king. One of the early Sangama rulers, Devaraya II, is reputed to have employed ten thousand Muslim horsemen. Abdul Razzaq reports that Devaraya II kept a copy of the Quran next to his throne so that his Muslim officers could take oaths of allegiance.

Nor was the Muslim population at Vijayanagara restricted to military personnel. In the fourteenth and fifteenth centuries, Arab traders were the principal importers of horses. The Vijayanagara king had a monopoly on the purchase of all these animals in southern India and attempted to control the activities of foreign horse traders. Reliefs on temples and ceremonial buildings at Vijayanagara depict Arab traders with long cloaks, pointed caps, and beards. Persians, too, came to Vijayanagara, and, as already noted, the first detailed accounts of life at the capital is by Abdul Razzaq. The presence of this emissary indicates the desire of the Vijayanagara rulers to maintain contacts with distant states, including those of the Islamic world. Builders and craftsmen of the Bahmani sultans may also have been brought to Vijayanagara to erect monuments within the royal center and elsewhere. Probably quite a few of these artisans were Muslim.

One Muslim quarter was situated on the northwest road within the walls of the urban core of the capital. Paes records that many Muslim inhabitants had been born in the region and were paid as members of the royal guard. Muslims must have tended gardens, for Paes describes a small river, perhaps an irrigation canal, below the quarter, where vineyards and orchards flourished. Other Muslim quarters of the capital were located in outlying settlements coinciding with the present-day village of Kadirampuram and the town of Hospet.

The principal architectural remains of Vijayanagara's Muslim quarters are funerary. The tombs that still stand are surrounded by gravestones, but none of these can be linked with known historical figures. The architecture of the Vijayanagara tombs is identical with that of those built in the Deccan under the patronage of the Bahmani sultans. Deccan Islamic techniques and styles were familiar at Vijayanagara from the end of the fourteenth century onwards. Two ruined mosques can be identified within the Muslim quarter of the urban core. They are noticeably un-Bahmani in appearance, since they make use of temple-like columns to support flat roofs; entrances are sheltered by angled eaves. An inscription in one mosque identifies the patron as Ahmad Khan, officer of Devaraya II. The domed tomb nearby was probably erected by this same officer.

Bahmani architectural influence at Vijayanagara extends beyond the Muslim quarters where, significantly, it is incorporated into the courtly architecture of the king's own residence. Pavilions, watchtowers, stables, and other buildings in the royal center at Vijayanagara are distinctive for their use of architectural techniques and forms derived from Deccan Islamic practice. These courtly structures are built of stone blocks set in thick mortar covered with plaster, now imperfectly preserved. Typical Bahmani-style features are arches with angled sides or with pointed or cusped profiles; vaults on square, octagonal, and even twelve-sided plans; and flattened domes with plain and fluted surfaces. The decoration of these buildings makes repeated use of the geometric patterns and stylized foliate motifs characteristic of Islamic art.

Despite the obvious Bahmani origin of such architectural elements, Vijayanagara's courtly architecture cannot truly be described as Islamic. Rather, it is a blend of two different traditions, Bahmani and southern Indian. Templelike features derived from southern India include double-curved eaves supported on brackets, pyramidal towers with ascending tiers of moldings, and ribbed or potlike finials. The creativity of the Vijayanagara builders is evident in the variety of building forms invented for courtly structures, no two of which are alike. These diverse architectural compositions contrast markedly with religious monuments, which are generally uniform within any one period. This fanciful courtly style expresses a culture which laid particular emphasis on display and pleasure. Many of these buildings must have been intended for royal reception and entertainment, both public and private.

The Bahmani-influenced courtly style at Vijayanagara also conveyed an ideological message, since the mixture of Islamic and indigenous features symbolized the cosmopolitan character of the capital and the universal pretensions of the king. Like the empire itself, which was composed of diverse peoples and cultures, Vijayanagara's courtly architecture blended disparate elements into a new and powerful synthesis.

Opposite: (30) Worn rock face of an overgrown roadway crossing the north ridge of the urban core.

Above: (31) Banana trees in the irrigated valley, with a temple at the foot of the rocky hill.

Below: (32) Cutting sugarcane in the fields outside Kadirampuram; ruined Islamic tombs are in the background.

Inside the Palace
In his palace within the gateways he is served by women and eunuchs and servants numbering fully five or six hundred; and these wives of the King all have their own officials for their service, but these are all women. The palaces of the King are large and with large rooms; they have cloisters like monasteries with cells, and in each one is one of his wives, and with each of these ladies is her maid-servant; and when the King retires to rest he passes through these cloisters, and his wives stand at the doors and call him.
Fernao Nuniz, Portuguese visitor to Vijayanagara, 1535-37

Opposite: (33) Once
filled with water, the
central court of the
square water pavilion in
the royal center is
overlooked by projecting
balconies.

Above: (34) Two-storied
octagonal pavilion,
possibly for receptions
and entertainments of
the king's private
household.

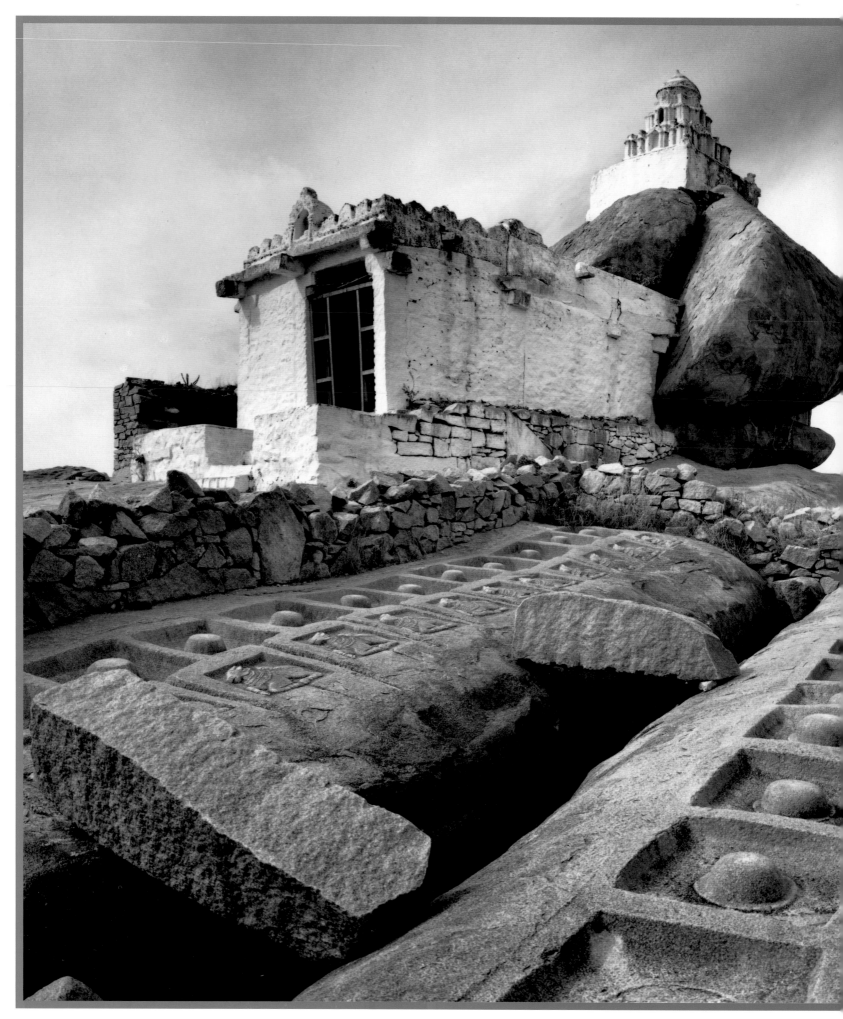

MYTHICAL LANDSCAPE

Vijayanagara's urban zones are defined, in part, by transitions in the surrounding landscape. The sacred center of the capital is situated in the most rugged part of the site, where the Tunghabadra flows in a northeasterly direction through a rocky gorge. Ridges in the urban core of the capital give way to valleys that open to the south and west, while the broad plain beyond is occupied by the outlying suburban centers of the metropolitan region. Through this coincidence of natural and urban forms, Vijayanagara's landscape was intrinsic to the growth of the city.

The legends and epic stories permeating Vijayanagara's natural setting evoke a sacred geography that gives meaning to the city. To begin, Pampa is the ancient name of a river, as recorded in local versions of the Ramayana epic, as well as being that of a goddess. Pampa is preserved in the name of Hampi (the "P" of old Kannada being replaced by "h" in the modern language) on the south bank of the river, the holy spot associated with this goddess. River, goddess, and the sacred center of the capital are all thus interrelated.

According to local myth, Pampa was the daughter of the sage Matanga. In order to express her devotion to Shiva, Pampa regularly offered fruits and flowers to the sages who gathered around the shrine of Virupaksha, the name by which Shiva is known at Hampi. Pleased with her service, the sages granted Pampa her wish to wed Virupaksha, instructing her in the appropriate rites of penance. Each day Pampa came down to the river to bathe, displaying herself to the god, who was impressed with her piety and no doubt also her beauty. Virupaksha bestowed his grace upon her and expressed his desire to marry. In order to persuade Matanga, he caused gold to rain on Hemakuta Hill as a dowry. Eventually, the divine couple were married in the presence of the gods and sages.

The betrothal and marriage ceremonies of Pampa and Virupaksha are commemorated each spring in the Virupaksha temple at Hampi. Thousands of pilgrims are in attendance on these occasions, as they were in the days of Vijayanagara. Daily worship of the god and goddess also takes place in the Virupaksha shrine, the oldest of the large religious complexes in the sacred center.

Shiva, as Virupaksha, was adopted by the first Vijayanagara rulers as the guardian deity of the dynasty; the god's name is quoted in early Vijayanagara inscriptions and copperplate grants of money or land. Some of the shrines on Hemakuta Hill overlooking Hampi, dating back to the centuries before the Vijayanagara era, are dedicated to Shiva. Yet it is Pampa who was the divinity orig-

(35) Rock-cut lingas and shrine built into a boulder on Malyavanta Hill form part of the cult of Shiva.

inally worshipped at Hampi. The Tungabhadra site is commonly referred to as Pampakshetra, the holy place of Pampa, where Virupaksha is Pampa's lord, Pampapati. In this respect, both god and site are defined in terms of the goddess. Some versions of the legend suggest that it was Pampa who first attracted Virupaksha to the Tungabhadra region. So it would seem that Hampi was first associated with Pampa and only later with Virupaksha. A vestige of the original importance of this goddess is the Pampa Sarovar, a pond near the north bank of the Tungabhadra. Hemakuta Hill, the abode of Shiva, is also linked with Matanga and Pampa.

Representations of Pampa and Virupaksha are confined to the Hampi complex, but the region is filled with sculptures depicting other aspects of Shiva. Images of Virabhadra, the ferocious, warriorlike form of the god, are carved on boulders and sometimes incorporated into small shrines. Such shrines are built at the summits of rocky outcrops, as on Matanga Hill and the ridge on the north side of the urban core. The most common manifestations of Shiva are the linga, the phallic emblem symbolizing the god's potency, and the bull mount, Nandi. Groups of lingas, some forming geometric diagrams or mandalas, are sculpted on the rocks beside the Tungabhadra; here, too, there are rock-cut Nandi images. Rows of lingas and Nandis carved in shallow relief line the sides of a natural cistern on Malyavanta Hill. Another image in Vijayanagara's landscape is Ganesha, the elephant-headed god. The widespread popularity of this deity arises from his power to ensure worshipers success in all their endeavors. Two large representations of Ganesha are hewn out of granite boulders on the elevated ridge to the south of Hampi; both are contained in shrines.

Episodes from the Ramayana story are closely linked with the Vijayanagara site. Local legends and inscriptions identify the surrounding landscape with Kishkindha, the mythical kingdom of the monkey chiefs Sugriva and Vali. According to the Ramayana, Sugriva and his monkey general, Hanuman, were driven out of Kishkindha by Sugriva's brother, Vali. They sought refuge near the home of Matanga, who had earlier placed a curse on Vali. Meanwhile, in the kingdom of Ayodhya far to the north, the rightful heir to the throne, Rama, had been banished to the forest together with his wife, Sita, and his brother, Lakshmana. Sita was abducted by the demon Ravana, and Rama and Lakshmana traveled southward to search for her. Arriving at the bank of the Pampa (described in a local version of the Ramayana as a river), they came across the monkey refugees. After listening to their story, Rama killed Vali, burning his body on a funeral pyre, and then restored Sugriva to the throne of Kishkindha. Sugriva and Hanuman, in gratitude, pledged the support

of the monkey army. They promised to find Sita and to bring her back safely to Rama. While Rama waited near Kishkindha, Hanuman discovered Sita in captivity in Lanka, the island kingdom of Ravana. On receiving Hanuman's news, Rama and Lakshmana planned the campaign to rescue Sita. They were helped by Jambavan, king of the bears, and by Hanuman; the monkey warriors built the stone bridge to Lanka. The climax of the story is the battle between Rama and Ravana; the demon is killed and Sita is rescued unharmed. This story concludes with the triumphant return of Rama to Ayodhya and his coronation as rightful king.

Various natural features at Vijayanagara are identified with the Ramayana narrative. A small pond near the south bank of the river, known as Sita Sarovar, is said to be where Sita bathed. In a rocky cleft nearby, Sugriva is believed to have hidden the jewels that Sita dropped when she was abducted in Ravana's aerial chariot. Streaks on a rocky shelf in front of the cleft are pointed out as marks made by the scarf in which Sita wrapped her jewels before they fell to earth. Matanga Hill was the residence of the sage who protected Sugriva and Hanuman. Lakshmana crowned Sugriva immediately beneath this hill, where the Tungabhadra turns northward. Rama waited on Malyavanta Hill while Hanuman explored Lanka. A mound of ash a short distance northeast of the site is believed to be the cremated remains of Vali. A cavern close to Pampa Sarovar, on the north bank of the Tungabhadra, is identified as the hermitage of the female ascetic Shabari, a devotee of Rama. Nearby Anjenadri Hill is considered the birthplace of Hanuman, while the black-faced and red-faced monkeys which scamper over the rocks of the site are treated as descendants of Vali and Sugriva, respectively. The tumbled masses of fallen rock which dot the site are sometimes explained as the remains of the material collected by the monkeys in order to the build the bridge to Lanka.

Temples and shrines dedicated to Rama and Hanuman affirm the Ramayana associations of the site. The Raghunatha temple on Malyavanta Hill, for instance, has as its principal focus of worship a natural boulder carved with the principal characters of the story: Rama, Sita, Lakshmana, and Hanuman. The Kondandarama temple beneath Matanga Hill marks the coronation site of Sugriva on the bank of the Tungabhadra; an impressive image of the crowned Rama is enshrined here. Elsewhere, images of Rama and Lakshmana are carved on boulders in the landscape. A temple associated with Jambavan is located on a mountain slope above Hospet. Sculptures of

Opposite: (36) Monolithic sculpture of Narasimha, fierce incarnation of Vishnu, in the sacred center.

50

Opposite: (37) Sculpted columns of the detached mandapa in the Tiruvengalanatha temple complex.

Above: (38) Small shrines on the sloping shelf of Hemakuta Hill belong mostly to the pre-Vijayanagara era.

Below: (39) Distant view of the principal gopura of the Virupaksha temple at Hampi, the sixteenth-century monument of Krishnadevaraya.

(40) Sculpted panels of Ramayana battle scenes on the walls of the **Ramachandra** temple.

RAMA'S VICTORY OVER RAVANA

Rama and Ravana dueled with arrows. One after another, Rama broke the bows out of Ravana's hands until ninety-nine were gone and only one remained. The Demon King shot arrows long and short, thick and thin, quick and slow, from close range or far away; but Rama's armor was hard and impenetrable, he was unharmed and many arrows melted away when he saw them come.

Ravana seized his mace of iron set with lapis stones and embellished with gold. He gripped the iron handle with four hands and swung as the chariots met. It was too soon and the blow fell on the charioteer and not Rama.

Then Ravana drew apart and stopped. He whirled his mace in a circle arising and dipping his heads. The mace went faster and faster. Matali drove to deceive Ravana's aim and Rama reached for Indra's weapon-racks. He took a spear, and held it in one hand and threw it. That great dart went at Ravana resonant and vibrating with sound, with a noise like the thunder of a rockslide, the dark world falling, Ravana falling . . .

And the Demon Lord let go his mace; it sped, and Rama stood in its way. Ravana's chariot turned to run.

Rama's spear broke Ravana's flagpole; the cloth-of-gold war-flag fell. Rama broke the ten arrows of the Rakshasa Empire, and when he did, the running demon car lost its rattle and clatter and its wheels turned on in mournful silence. The flag of Lanka lay in the dust.

Rama opened a long bamboo case at his belt and took out the brass-bladed grass arrow given to him by Agastya, and notched it on his bowstring. That arrow could rend walls and gateways of stone; it breathed and sighed. Rama pulled his bow. He took three aiming steps backwards and held his breath. That was then the destined time and true setting of Ravana's death. Rama thought— "I must believe it! Oh kill him!"—

Rama shot. The bowstring rang out, all over the Universe. The arrow first broke the sword and bow Ravana raised to ward it, then it hit Ravana's breast and struck through his heart, stealing his life, and never stopped, but came out from his back and entered the Earth.

Down from Ravana's hands fell his broken bow and sword, and the Demon King of Lanka fell dying in his own dark form.

At first Rama didn't move. Then he first unstrung his bow and put it aside. Then he lifted Matali into Indra's rain-chariot and the misty horses rose running through the sky and were gone. At daybreak, at dawn, Ravana died.

Climactic battle scene from the *Ramayana*.

Hanuman are commonly placed inside shrines, on fortification and gateway walls, and along roads and pathways. Some of the city's lookouts are named after this legendary hero; one lookout is inscribed the "bastion of Hanuman."

Today, the Ramayana geography of Vijayanagara is narrated in locally printed manuals and brochures sold to devotees and visitors at Hampi. Small shrines, many with Rama or Hanuman carvings, define a pilgrimage route winding through the hills and along the river. The same texts also describe the natural features of the site in terms of Pampa and Virupaksha. In fact, the two mythologies overlap. At the betrothal of the god and goddess, for example, Rama is considered the brother of the bride; the wedding negotiations take place at the Kondandarama temple. In this way, the landscape itself coordinates the different stories. The sage Matanga, moreover, appears in both legends, first as the father of Pampa and, according to the Ramayana, as the protector of Sugriva and Hanuman. Matanga Hill, named after this sage, is the highest point within the city. Yet if the Pampa-Virupaksha legend lies at the core of the sacred center of the capital, the Ramayana epic pervades the whole site, both sacred center and urban core.

Vijayanagara's plan, in particular the spatial arrangement of the royal center, expresses the role of Rama as the creative force or center of the king's domain. As already noted, the elaborate temple of Ramachandra in the middle of this zone is the hub of inward and outward movement. Furthermore, the principal sanctuary of this temple is positioned on a north-south axis that passes through the middle of the royal center. This axis is marked by enclosure walls and roadways and is visually realized by the alignment of the temple's north porch with Matanga Hill, more than one kilometer to the north. Another visual alignment connects the temple's east porch with Malyavanta Hill to the northeast. Since both Matanga and Malyavanta are identified with particular Ramayana episodes, such alignments link Rama to the sites of his epic adventures.

Rama's creative energy is also expressed in the functional division of the royal center. The enclosures on either side of the north-south axis that passes through the Ramachandra temple accommodate different aspects of the king's life. The enclosures east of the axis constitute a zone of royal performance, providing the settings for the public and ceremonial activities of the king and of those in his service. The enclosures west of the axis, which constitute the zone of royal residence, contain the Virupaksha shrine of the king's private household and a number of palace structures. Since Ramachandra's sanctuary is located on the axis dividing these two zones, the god may be understood to both transcend and resolve the distinctions between the public and private domains of the ruler.

Vishnu is also included in Vijayanagara's sacred geography, though he is of considerably less significance. Rocks beside the Tungabhadra are carved with diverse representations of this deity, including an image of the god reclining on a serpent and a set of twenty-four multiple aspects. The most remarkable of Vishnu's appearances at Vijayanagara, however, is the lion-headed Narasimha sculpted out of a gigantic boulder midway between the sacred and royal centers. This is the largest and most demonic figure at the site; it has a head endowed with fiercely protruding eyes and a lionlike mouth. A diminutive goddess was once seated on the god's lap.

Innumerable shrines dedicated to different Hindu cults and occasionally also to saviors of the Jain religion dot the Vijayanagara region. Such structures are particularly concentrated in the sacred center of the capital but are by no means confined to this zone; they line the principal roads and gateways throughout the site and crown the summits of rocky hills. Temples were generally built of stone and are for this reason among the best-preserved structures at Vijayanagara. Some temples have inscriptions incised onto basements and walls, mostly in the southern Indian languages of Kannada and Telugu as well as a few in Sanskrit. These records are of particular interest since they name the temple donor, the gifts that he or she offered, and the date or reign of the ruling monarch. Such historical information is invaluable in reconstructing the temporal sequence of religious monuments, the deities to which they were dedicated, and the political and economic circumstances of the period.

The profusion of temples bears witness to the sanctity of the Vijayanagara site, the sustained patronage of religious cults by the courtly elite, and the widespread worship of gods and goddesses by virtually all the city's population. Devotion to Hindu divinities or Jain saviors was not merely an act of piety; it expressed the identity of the different peoples who served in the court and army and who were at the capital either permanently or temporarily. Particular cults were sponsored by the distinctive regional, ethnic, and linguistic groups who populated the capital.

Larger religious structures at Vijayanagara were generally erected by the rulers themselves, members of the royal family, ministers, and powerful military commanders. Smaller religious structures at Vijayanagara were supported by other influential figures in the court and army or by guilds and other professional associations. Thus, for instance, a late-fourteenth-century shrine east of the royal center was erected by a minister who was a follower of the

Jain religion. The northeast road that proceeds through the royal center toward the Ramachandra temple is lined with numerous shrines dedicated to diverse Hindu and Jain cults. These structures may have been erected by individuals or groups who wished to have their personal deities or saviors represented within the king's domain.

Temples at Vijayanagara sometimes served as memorials. An early-fourteenth-century example on Hemakuta has an inscription stating that its three Shiva lingas were established by Vira Kampiladeva, a local chief, in memory of his father, mother, and a third individual. In later times, important religious complexes were erected to commemorate particular occasions. The Krishna complex in the sacred center was founded by Krishnadevaraya to celebrate his military successes in the eastern Deccan over the Gajapati rulers of Orissa. Coronations, too, could be occasions for lavish benefactions to temples. Krishnadevaraya made generous donations to the Virupaksha temple when he ascended the throne. It is possible that the Anantashayana temple outside Hospet was endowed by the same ruler when his son formally became heir apparent.

Religious complexes at Vijayanagara were maintained by grants of money, gold, and other precious items, as well as by income from villages and cultivated land. Economic transactions detailed in temple inscriptions suggest that these institutions indirectly administered land, water, and crops. Unlike the king and members of court and army, who usually spent many months away from the capital, temple priests permanently resided in the city. They supervised such agricultural projects, and it is no coincidence that many larger temples are situated near irrigated fields and reservoirs. Stores to house gold and other valuables were built inside temple complexes. An unusual example is the multidomed granary inside the Krishna temple of the sacred center.

Brahmin specialists advised on appropriate temple rites, ceremonies, and festivities. Elaborate temple rituals required large numbers of employees, from expounders of sacred texts to dancers and musicians to bearers of standards, lamps, and flowers. A network of suppliers kept temples stocked with grain, flowers, oil, sandalwood, and other essential items. At the Virupaksha complex in Hampi, the only large shrine still in use at Vijayanagara, a glimpse may be had of the daily activities of brahmins and other temple employees. The complex incorporates kitchens, dining areas, and stores, as well as a police station and even a post office. Nearby is a matha, or monastery, where learned brahmins and students are accommodated.

Feeding of brahmins was an important ritual for the Vijayanagara kings, a measure of both personal piety and public sponsorship of religious establishments. The giving of gifts to brahmins was sometimes also a ceremonial occasion. Outside the Vithala temple, near the pathway that follows the south bank of the Tungabhadra, is a simple stone structure from which a metal balance was once suspended. According to popular tradition, the king was here weighed against jewels and gold, which were then distributed to brahmins. (More likely, however, the balance served as a swing for deities on certain festival days.)

At the core of each Vijayanagara temple is a small sanctuary known as the garbhagriha, or womb chamber. This housed the stone and metal images which were the principal focus of devotion. Smaller shrines had only a single sanctuary, whereas larger temples usually had two or more shrines integrated into a single complex or built as separate structures. Multiple sanctuaries permitted the worship of the principal temple divinity along with his female consort and a host of minor gods. Temple sanctuaries were plain and dark, with oil lamps providing dim illumination. Only brahmin priests were permitted to enter the sanctuary to execute the appropriate rites. Devotees stood before the doorway in order to catch an auspicious glimpse, known as darshana, of the divinity. They also may have paid homage to the deity by proceeding around the shrine in a clockwise direction, a rite known as pradakshina. Narrow passageways around three sides of the sanctuaries in the larger Vijayanagara temples were for the auspicious circumabulations of worshipers.

Throughout the fourteenth century, both before and immediately after the foundation of Vijayanagara, temple exteriors were generally austere, in conformance with local Deccan practice. From the fifteenth century onward, however, temple designs were increasingly influenced by techniques and traditions derived from the Tamil region, and these were eventually assimilated to become the characteristic Vijayanagara style. The walls of temples in this Tamil-influenced style are divided into bays by regularly spaced shallow pilasters. The central niches flanked by pairs of similar pilasters were intended for sculpted stone panels, but almost none of these remain at Vijayanagara. The carvings on the Ramachandra shrine in the royal center, as on several other temples, also cover the wall surface between pilasters.

The towers which rise over the sanctuaries of earlier temples at Vijayanagara are stone pyramidal compositions, with ascending tiers of deeply cut horizontal moldings. Towers on temples of the fifteenth and sixteenth centuries in the typical Vijayanagara style, however, are constructed in brick. They have successive stories, diminishing in height as they ascend, each with pilastered walls and miniature towered forms creating false parapets. The towers are capped with hemispherical, domed, or rectangular

Above: (41) Ganagitti Jain temple, an early-styled temple erected by a king's minister.

Below: (42) The eastern gopura of the Raghunatha temple complex is built close to a boulder on Malyavanta Hill.

Above: (43) Tiruvengalanatha temple in the southeastern part of the royal center.

Below: (44) Nighttime at the entrance to the Krishna temple complex in the sacred center; pilgrims pass by on their way to Hampi.

vaulted roofs. Plaster decoration enlivens the architectural elements with monster faces and exuberant foliate motifs. Plaster figures of gods and semidivine creatures are placed in the upper stories.

One or more columned halls, or mandapas, precede the sanctuaries of larger Vijayanagara temples. The mandapas of fourteenth- and early-fifteenth-century temples are massive and plain, but they are greatly elaborated in the sixteenth century. The columns of these later halls generally have cubic blocks covered with carvings of deities and sacred emblems; other supporting elements are fashioned with considerable virtuosity into clusters of colonettes surrounding a central shaft or into rearing lionlike beasts known as yalis. Brackets are curved with a simple pendant lotus at the end; those on the outside are sheltered by elegant, double-curved eaves. Above the eaves are brick parapets with niches having cusped arches and miniature templelike towers. The plaster figures that filled the niches and the monster masks that ornamented their frames have mostly been lost. The plaster was brightly painted, but much of the original color work has faded. Of the painted compositions that once adorned the ceilings of mandapas, only that in the Virupaksha temple has survived intact. This large mural is divided symmetrically into panels, many filled with a figure of Shiva with attendant deities.

The largest sixteenth-century temples at Vijayanagara generally have two mandapas aligned on an east-west axis. The inner hall is square and enclosed by walls with doorways sheltered by a porch; the outer hall is open, usually with projections in the middle of three sides. Open, freestanding structures functioned as wedding halls, or kalyana mandapas. These accommodated annual festivals enacting the marriages of gods and their consorts. During these ceremonies, sacred images of deities were displayed on a raised dais within the hall. Subsidiary structures within temple complexes include small altars with lotuslike designs on the top and open pavilions for the animal or bird mounts (such as Nandi for Shiva and Garuda for Vishnu) on which the deity sometimes rode. Columns holding lamps are either brass-covered wooden posts or monoliths hewn out of single stone blocks.

All these shrines, mandapas, altars, and lamp columns are contained within rectangular, paved courtyards and surrounded by colonnades which abut the high enclosure walls. The Krishna and Tiruvengalanatha complexes in the sacred center each has two sets of concentric walls. Enclosures are entered through towered gateways known as gopuras, which are aligned with the mandapas or prin-

(45) The double enclosures of the Tiruvengalanatha temple complex from the summit of Matanga Hill, with the chariot street running northward to the Tungabhadra.

60

Coronation Ceremony

All the commanders and ministers came together for the occasion, as well as scholars of the city, not to mention the astrologers, great poets, and other people both young and old. All of them together helped to give Krishnaraya the ritual bath at an auspicious moment, just as it is prescribed in the Shastras. Then they had him sit on a gold seat on the ceremonial platform, where he performed the sixteen great donations.

From the *Rayavachakamu*, a contemporary courtly epic

Opposite: (46) Ritual
bath in the largest
enclosure of the royal
center, a recent
discovery by the
Archaeological Survey of
India.

Below: (47) Overgrown
bathing tank of the
Krishna temple complex
in the sacred center.

63

Above: (48) Columned mandapas facing into the courtyard of the Vithala temple complex in the sacred center.

Below: (49) Stone imitation of a ceremonial chariot used as a shrine for Garuda in the Vithala temple.

Opposite: (50) Minor shrine, gateway, and colonnade with frangipani tree in the Vithala temple courtyard.

Chariot Festival

Outside the city walls on the north there are three very beautiful pagodas, one of which is called Vitella. Whenever the festival of any of these temples occurs they drag along certain triumphal cars which run on wheels, and with it go dancing-girls and other women with music to the temple, conducting the idol along the said street with much pomp.

DOMINGO PAES, Portuguese visitor to Vijayanagara, 1520-22

cipal shrines. Gopuras are higher and more imposing than sanctuary towers and are, therefore, the dominant architectural features. Entrance gateways in fifteenth-century temples are simple structures with doorways flanked by open porches and overhung by angled eaves. By the sixteenth century, the earlier Tamil gopura scheme had been adopted at Vijayanagara. The typical gopura is a massive structure with a double-storied, granite lower portion, above which rises a pyramid of hollow brickwork on a wooden framework. Diminishing stories have pilastered walls and false parapets with openings in the middle of the front and back sides; vaulted roofs at the summits have arched ends and potlike finials. Most of the painted plaster figures and decoration which adorned these brick towers have now vanished.

The great sixteenth-century complexes at Vijayanagara are approached along ceremonial streets. These run eastward from the Virupaksha, Krishna, and Vithala complexes but northward from the Tiruvengalanatha complex. Paved in stone, these long streets were used by chariots bearing images of the gods on festival occasions. These vehicles were pulled by devotees from the main gopuras of the temples to small shrines or mandapas at the ends of the thoroughfares, the turning points for the chariots. Such ceremonies were extremely popular since the great crowds of worshipers which assembled on these occasions could benefit from an auspicious view of the temple deities. Chariots are still pulled along the Hampi temple street each spring to celebrate the betrothal and marriage festivities of Virupaksha and Pampa. The colonnades and other structures that line the Hampi street were used by religious leaders and members of the court as viewing stands. Merchants were also accommodated here since temple festivals were great markets. Jewels, ritual items, and refreshments were sold in small shops set into the colonnades. Today, as in ancient times, the Hampi street is referred to as a bazaar because of the many shops and restaurants that flourish there.

Bathing was essential for worship, and many shrines in the sacred center at Vijayanagara were located near the Tungabhadra. For those complexes situated away from the river, natural or rock-cut reservoirs were often necessary. All the great sixteenth-century complexes have large rectangular bathing tanks located beside the colonnaded streets. These reservoirs are lined with stone steps on four sides and have pavilions standing in the middle of the water. At certain times of the year, ceremonial images were carried in procession to tanks where they were gently placed in floating shrines.

(51) Sculpted piers with rearing beasts and clustered colonettes inside the main hall of the Vithala temple complex.

A FRAGILE HERITAGE

During the seventeenth and eighteenth centuries, almost no foreign visitors traveled to the ruins of Vijayanagara. That the site continued to be pillaged by seekers of treasure and construction materials is suggested by vandalized buildings and the dearth of precious items in the recent archaeological excavations. Yet knowledge about Vijayanagara must have been been preserved, for scholarly investigation was initiated relatively early, in December 1799, by Colonel Colin Mackenzie. This energetic antiquarian, later surveyor general of India, was the first modern investigator to describe the layout of Vijayanagara. Mackenzie took considerable pains to identify ruined structures, noting temples dedicated to different Hindu deities, extensive irrigation works, and lines of fortification walls. His report, is now in the collection of the India Office Library and Records, London.

Though Mackenzie's pioneer documentation was never published, curiosity about Vijayanagara was awakened. By 1836, the first description of the site had appeared, accompanied by translations of temple inscriptions. An expedition to Vijayanagara in the same year, led by the Frenchman Edouard de Warren, was cut short by an outbreak of malaria. Despite this and other hazards, many visitors made the journey to Vijayanagara throughout the nineteenth century. They were attracted by the remarkable setting of the ruins, with its breathtaking views of the Tungabhadra River and the surrounding hills of rugged granite. Travelers generally remarked on the splendor of the temples and their exquisite carvings, the unusual compositions of courtly buildings such as the elephant stables and the gigantic stone blocks of the fortifications.

Undoubtedly it was the promise of picturesque ruins within a spectacular landscape that lured the first photographers to Vijayanagara. Their journey to what was then a remote site was hampered by cumbersome photographic boxes and chemicals. Recently, sixty waxed-paper negatives taken in 1856 by Colonel Alexander Greenlaw were discovered in England. Greenlaw's negatives are outstanding examples of the early art of photography; more important, they constitute the most comprehensive nineteenth-century survey of the site, recording valuable building details that have long ago vanished. The first published photographs of Vijayanagara appeared in 1866 in *Architecture in Dharwar and Mysore*. Accompanying captions were contributed by the prominent architectural historian James Fergusson, who regretted that he was unable personally to visit the site.

(52) Blocks from an overturned temple mandapa on the northeast road in the royal center.

In 1880 the Madras Survey issued the first topographic map of Vijayanagara, with identifying labels for the monuments. Inscriptions on the temples also began to be copied and translated at about this time. At the turn of the century the viceroy of India, Lord Curzon, made a grant for the conservation of the Vijayanagara monuments. The Madras office of the newly founded Archaeological Survey began to clear the buildings of cactus and accumulated earth and to prop up collapsing walls and doorway lintels. Watchmen were appointed to guard the monuments, and attempts were made to reveal buried structures. Despite all these efforts, progress was hindered by the destructive effects of vegetation and by repeated outbreaks of malaria.

The first director of these operations, A. L. Longhurst, was the first expert archaeologist to work at Vijayanagara. In 1917 he brought out *Hampi Ruins*, a guidebook that summarized his firsthand knowledge of the site. Here, Longhurst outlined the historical and archaeological context of Vijayanagara, systematically describing the fortifications and irrigation works, civic and ceremonial structures, temples, and sculptures. By the time Longhurst's guidebook appeared, the first detailed history of Vijayanagara had already been published. Robert Sewell's *A Forgotten Empire*, dating from 1900, was a historical synthesis of all known inscriptions and manuscripts. To this masterly survey of Vijayanagara's history were appended the first English translations of the chronicles of the Portuguese travelers Domingo Paes and Fernao Nuniz. Interest in Vijayanagara was greatly stimulated by these contemporary descriptions, which vividly portrayed life in the city at the height of its power and influence.

By the mid-1920s, Vijayanagara was neither forgotten nor ignored. Its importance as a symbol of Indian creative force grew. General studies on Indian town planning and architecture and the social and political life of the Vijayanagara empire frequently referred to the city, especially its urban layout and principal monuments. Even so, conservation and research at Vijayanagara during the following decades lost something of its initial impetus. Efforts continued to be made to prevent the collapse of large standing monuments and to clear the encroaching vegetation, but little was published concerning the architecture at the site.

The 1970s witnessed a resurgence of interest in Vijayanagara, partly inspired by D. Devakunjari's excellent guidebook, issued by the Archaeological Survey in 1970 and reprinted several times. This thorough description of the site cautiously interprets the functions of the different zones of the city while proposing a chronology for the more important buildings. Innovative research during this decade was undertaken by Pierre and Vasundhara Filliozat of the French Institute of Indian Studies. They concentrated on the Vithala temple, which they measured in de-

tail, photographing the sculptures and translating the many inscriptions. These scholars also examined the overall plan of the city, identifying different quarters, markets, and streets.

In the mid-1970s, Indian archaeologists turned their attention to Vijayanagara under a newly conceived national project for the investigation of three medieval cities. Excavations at the Vijayanagara site were initiated by teams from the Archaeological Survey of India and the Department of Archaeology and Museums of the Government of Karnataka, the state in which Vijayanagara is located. The former team was at first led by Dr. S. R. Rao, while the latter team was directed by Dr. M. S. Nagaraja Rao later director general of the Archaeological Survey. The ongoing Vijayanagara excavations have uncovered the foundations of civic and residential structures in the royal center. Epigraphic investigation on the part of the state archaeological team has identified many new inscriptions. The results of this research are embodied in the *Progress of Research* volumes regularly issued by the Government of Karnataka Department of Archaeology and Museums.

The contribution of the international team of scholars and students to the study of Vijayanagara began in January 1980 under George Michell and, from 1981 onward, John M. Fritz. The team consisted of archaeologists, architects, art historians, and photographers assembled from Australia, Great Britain, Germany, and the United States, as well as from India. Initially, these volunteer workers prepared drawings and photographs for a 1982 issue of *Marq*, the popular Indian art magazine, an issue of which was devoted to Vijayanagara in 1982. Fieldwork in subsequent seasons developed into a major research project that has been sustained throughout the 1980s.

The early work of the international team documented cultural features over a large area of Vijayanagara's site. To determine the form and extent of the city's layout, a sketch map was prepared of an area of about twenty-five square kilometers by using existing aerial photographs and corrective ground checks. Since the mid-1980s, a professional surveying team from Bangalore has been preparing detailed topographic maps for the central part of Vijayanagara. These maps locate buildings and other archaeological features—such as lines of fortifications, water channels, and aqueducts—and the routes of roads and pathways.

Because of the participation of architects and architecture students, the international team was able to carry out an extensive program of measured drawing. Over the years plans, elevations, and sections were completed for almost all the major monuments at the site, religious, ceremonial, and courtly. Sculpted balustrades and columns of

(53) Opposite: Five-storied, towered gopura of the Pattabhirama temple Complex near Kamalapuram.

Above: (54) Rubble and collapsing enclosure walls in the royal center; the square watchtower is in the distance.

Below: (55) Defaced Nandi at the end of the Hampi bazaar.

Above: (56) Abandoned Vaishnava temple complex on the northeast road in the royal center.

Below: (57) Water buffalo on their way past the Ganesha temple on the ridge above Hampi, with the gopura of the Virupaksha temple beyond.

unusual interest were recorded in detail. Photography played a crucial role in this project, providing evocations of the romantic setting of the site as well as systematic records of architecture and sculpture.

Of the many buildings at Vijayanagara pillaged and burned by the conquerors or subsequently abandoned to weather and vandals, some are partly buried while others are eroded almost beyond recognition. Techniques of "surface archaeology" were developed by the international team in order to study these fragmentary remains. Within the royal enclosures, for example, indications of all structural activity, no matter how slight, were described and photographed. Architects, under the supervision of archaeologists, measured archaeological features such as rubble walls and stone column bases partly visible in the earth and vegetation. Overturned blocks, rock-cut postholes and other barely noticeable features were also recorded, as were the remains of structures recently exposed by the Indian excavators. This documentation has revealed the varied forms of a long-hidden architectural tradition.

The international team has also examined earthenware ceramics discovered in the excavations and hydraulic works that provided water for civic, domestic, and agricultural uses. An ongoing archaeological reconnaissance of the metropolitan region of Vijayanagara is examining patterns of settlement in the outlying zones of the capital. Of particular concern in this study are the nature of craft production associated with the city and the types of crops that were grown to feed both people and animals. Such research attempts to locate the material remains of Vijayanagara within its social and economic context. Among the problems to be tackled are the identification and distribution of different peoples within the city and the physical and commercial connections between the capital and its surrounding districts.

But Vijayanagara has also to be understood within its historical perspective. Over the past two decades, historians have developed new interpretations of the state-formation process during the Vijayanagara period and the ritual roles of kings at the capital. The international team has recruited literary experts to examine the quasi-historical documents of the period. Some texts include descriptions of courtly life at the capital, detailing the careers of kings and military commanders. Other texts are compilations of legends pertaining to the sacred geography of the Vijayanagara region. The perspectives of different scholars working with both historical and archaeological documents challenge long-held views of the site and open possibilities for a new and increasingly sophisticated understanding of Vijayanagara.

Documentation of Vijayanagara by Indian archaeologists and the international team has not been completed, nor can it be completed in the foreseeable future. Extensive sites like Vijayanagara require the energies and imagination of more than one generation of scholars. Research at Vijayanagara by both Indian and international experts will be continued in the years to come.

Future investigation assumes the adequate protection of the Vijayanagara site; but, like so many other ancient places throughout the world, Vijayanagara is at risk. Until recently, the region of the Vijayanagara site was remote and underpopulated; in the official reports of the British it was usually described as "backward." The building of the great dam across the Tungabhadra, a short distance southwest of the site, was among the largest hydroelectric projects of the postindependence era, which completely transformed the Tungabhadra valley after the 1950s. Today, irrigation permits extensive cultivation of rice, bananas, and sugarcane. Reliable electricity has encouraged the growth of local industry. Hospet is now a thriving provincial town of no fewer than one hundred thousand inhabitants. Iron ore is mined in the hills nearby; a site to the east has been set aside for a steel mill. Direct train connections between Hospet, Bangalore, Hyderabad, and Goa—as well as improved bus services—mean that the Vijayanagara site is increasingly accessible to visitors. The construction of new hotels in Hospet and Kamalapuram, on the edge of the Vijayanagara site, allows growing numbers of tourists.

The ruins of greater Vijayanagara encompass more than 250 square kilometers that constitute a region of increased agricultural development and expanding population. It is hardly surprising, therefore, that the archaeological remains survive in a range of varying conditions. A limited number of individual monuments benefit from the direct protection of the Archaeological Survey of India or from the Government of Karnataka Department of Archaeology and Museums, the two agencies that respectively represent the central and state governments. These authorities have been undertaking architectural conservation, much of which is of a rescue nature. The work ranges from stabilizing collapsing structures and disintegrating sculptures, to partial rebuilding and replacement of building elements.

Conservation of standing monuments and sculptures is not the only concern of the archaeological authorities. In more recent years they have embarked upon excavations in the royal center. Buried strata in the enclosures of this zone contain masonry foundations of civic, ceremonial, and residential structures as well as stone debris and artifacts. Techniques of stratigraphic excavation have disclosed layers formed during the occupation and destruction of the city. Some artifacts in these layers have been systematically collected, documented, and analyzed to provide information on the history and uses of particular areas and structures.

These excavations are accompanied by a conservation

program which aims at stabilizing fragile plaster elements and eroding earthen floors. Such work, however, has not always been thorough. Plaster figures uncovered in a palace structure excavated in the late 1970s, for instance, have not survived exposure to the elements. The archaeologists have dismantled and reconstructed some of these fragmentary remains, and several platforms and basements have been rebuilt. In the early 1970s a museum was erected in the nearby village of Kamalapuram to display loose carvings and other objects of interest taken from the ruins. A large-scale model of the site, complete with miniature granite boulders and flowing water for the Tungabhadra, occupies its central courtyard.

Unfortunately, most of the Vijayanagara site is not under the jurisdiction of the central or state governments, whose authority is restricted to the limited areas occupied by individual monuments and excavation trenches. A large proportion of the urban core is unprotected as a result, and many temple complexes, small shrines, mosques, tombs, wells, and other unidentified but visible structures remain unlisted. Lines of fortification walls and water channels, as well as dams and other indicators of Vijayanagara-period building activity, are similarly unnoted. Architectural monuments and hydraulic features in the outlying settlements are mostly unprotected. Deposits containing the remains of ruined buildings and artifacts used in and near them are ignored.

The archaeological authorities do not have jurisdiction over most of these remains. Substantial areas of the Vijayanagara site are owned by local farmers, whose industry over the years has increased with the availability of water from the Tungabhadra dam. In their eagerness to grow crops, these farmers have not always respected the fabric of ancient structures. Temples and columned halls have been dismantled to increase the size of arable fields or dislodged by the softening of the earth as water is introduced for irrigation. Foundations of ruined structures and their accompanying artifacts have been cleared to make way for fields. Fill has been removed from fortifications and buildings to increase land elevation. Rubble walls and artifacts associated with buildings have been piled to the sides of fields or carted away; stone blocks have been pillaged for building materials. New pathways and water channels breach the walls.

Unauthorized reuse of ancient structures has occurred throughout the Vijayanagara region. With the increase in the local population following the reintroduction of irrigation in the area, and the growing popularity of Hampi as a pilgrimage site, many shrines have been renovated and resident priests installed. Though this is particularly evident within the sacred center, shrines elsewhere in the site are once again being used as places of worship. This revival of interest leads to the application of whitewash to columns and walls and the adornment of sculptures with brightly colored paint. In some cases, such as the Raghunatha temple on Malyavanta Hill, a major religious complex, priests have taken charge and are now permanently settled. Other dilapidated structures throughout the site are used as rest houses for pilgrims or as monasteries for visiting holy men and their disciples. Tombs within the Muslim quarters in the urban core continue to be venerated, the gravestones being whitewashed and covered with traditional green cloth.

Nor are all the new residents at Vijayanagara priests and pilgrims. The colonnades that line the bazaar street of the Virupaksha temple at Hampi, for instance, are being increasingly occupied by poorly paid laborers and their families. Such squatters claim the ancient structures as their own, burning fires in the roadway and hanging up washing between ancient columns. Other colonnades within the bazaar accommodate restaurants and shops that serve visitors to the Virupaksha shrine. As the number of pilgrims has increased, so too have these facilities. Freshly painted storefronts, steadily encroaching onto the roadway, envelop the original structures. Regrettably, some sections of the colonnades have been dismantled in recent years to make way for new construction.

Where extant ancient structures are no longer available for the ever-growing numbers of residents and visitors to the Vijayanagara site, new ones have been erected. A wealthy Jain establishment has constructed a number of large concrete buildings in recent years, disfiguring the prominent ridge that overlooks Hampi from the south. Several small structures on Hemakuta Hill have recently been demolished to provide space for a new ashram. In the villages marking the original outlying settlements of Vijayanagara there is a noticeable increase in house construction that obliterates any evidence of past use. Hospet, the largest town in the region, has grown rapidly in recent years, obscuring all existing traces of Krishnadevaraya's residence. Houses at Anegondi, on the north bank of the Tungabhadra, either incorporate ancient structures or abut directly against their walls.

The modification of the Vijayanagara site is not restricted to archaeological remains. The landscape itself is being vandalized. The remarkable natural setting of the city is as much a part of the ancient heritage as the monuments themselves; it too needs protection. The availability of granite, the preferred structural material for houses and factories, has proved irresistible to local contractors. There has been extensive quarrying of granite by laborers who, in the last few years, have turned to dynamite as the most convenient method of splitting rock.

The problems faced by Vijayanagara are in no way unique. Similar, if not graver, risks are faced by innumerable archaeological sites throughout the world. But Vi-

Opposite: (58) Children
in the Hampi bazaar.
The dilapidated
colonnades in the
background are now
lived in by local workers.

Above: (59) Gateway at
Malpannagudi, now a
garage for the temple
chariot, on the road from
Hospet to Hampi.

Below: (60) Tower of
the Anantashayana
temple rising above
thatched workers' huts
on the outskirts of
Hospet.

Above: (61) Fortified gateway leading to the citadel above Anengondi. The part-circular bastions are post-Vijayanagara in date.

Below: (62) U-shaped courtly pavilion standing below the canal that runs along the south side of the Irrigated Valley.

Opposite: (63) Recently excavated palace structures in the royal center; only the foundations, floors, and lower portions of the walls are preserved.

Palaces of the King and His Lords
Here always dwells the king, and here he has great and fair palaces, in
which he always lodges, with many enclosed courts and great houses very well
built, and within them wide open spaces, with water tanks in great numbers,
in which is reared an abundance of fish. In the city as well there are palaces
after the same fashion, wherein dwell the great Lords and Governors thereof.
DUARTE BARBOSA, Portuquese visitor to Vijayanagara, 1518

jayanagara offers an important opportunity for archaeologists, since only in the last few decades has the pace of human alteration of the site greatly increased. There is still time to study Vijayanagara and to rescue it from the perils of future unplanned development. An informed and considered master plan for conserving Vijayanagara could be a model for other sites in India and usable even in other countries where there are extensive remains of ruined cities.

No master plan for the protection and conservation of Vijayanagara can be conceived without an understanding of what constitutes the ancient zone. A complete map of the region locating all archaeological features is needed, as is an inventory providing detailed descriptions. As a counterpart to this documentation of visible ancient features, some estimate must be made of that which is no longer visible but which must still exist beneath the ground. Raised mounds of earth, varying patterns of vegetation, and alignments of standing structures may all be indicators of buried structures. The condition and historical significance of archaeological desposits and of buried and standing structures has to be evaluated. Some concept of the future directions of archaeological investigation needs to be formulated. Which new developments in excavation methods and conservation techniques, for example, might effectively be applied at this site? "Surface archaeology" techniques used by the international team at Vijayanagara have already proved their use.

Ideally, authorities would be involved with all activities that affect the material remains of the Vijayanagara region, authorized or not. The agricultural life of the Tungabhadra valley is not likely to decline. Thus it is imperative that landowners and laborers be educated about standing structures and buried deposits so that they may help to preserve, rather than destroy, their ancient heritage. Agriculturists have already demonstrated how water features may be reused: canals, dams, and bridges dating from the Vijayanagara period are maintained by farmers who rely on a constant supply of water. Agricultural reuse of the land need not always be in conflict with archaeological conservation.

Priests and pilgrims can be shown how to reuse ancient temples and shrines without causing damage. After all, such buildings were designed for worship in the past, and there is no reason why their stone fabric cannot withstand additional use. Whitewashing structures and painting sculptures need not cause corrosion if the right materials and methods can be found. As for the squatters and merchants who reside in the colonnades of the Hampi bazaar, they too must be persuaded to treat these structures with

(64) King's balance, probably a swing for images of gods on festival occasions, and gateway near the Vithala temple complex in the sacred center.

respect. Since such colonnades were originally intended to accommodate similar activities, there is once again good reason for reconciling present-day needs with preservation of the past. Deposits containing Vijayanagara-period remains should be carefully excavated before construction begins.

To handle the number of visitors to the site, including both pilgrims and tourists, basic facilities have to be provided. At this time, restaurants offer limited food, and safe drinking water is almost unobtainable. There is little point in searching for a public toilet. Buses and cars carrying visitors proceed through the middle of the ruins, passing dangerously close to ancient structures, with which they sometimes collide. There is no bus stand at the site, and travelers must wait in the sun for irregular services. Accommodation within the ancient area of Vijayanagara is limited to a few bare rooms managed by the Virupaksha temple in the sacred center, as well as several nearby mathas. Local tourist authorities have recently completed a small hotel in Kamalapuram, but this is unlikely to meet future needs. In 1982 the Government of Karnataka created the Hampi Authority, a high-level commission intended to coordinate the activities of all agencies that affect the historic Vijayanagara area. The Hampi Authority meets regularly and considers a variety of proposals. It has conceived a "Hampi Resurrection Project" to restore the former glory of the site and has attempted to stop quarrying and unauthorized construction. In 1988 a "Hampi Heritage Conservation and Development plan" was prepared for the Karnataka State Tourist Development Corporation. The plan recognizes the competing and sometimes conflicting demands of archaeological preservation and exploration, tourism and pilgrimage, agriculture and industry. It recommends that the Vijayanagara region be divided into different zones with varying intensities of conservation and development.

When this or other future programs of conservation and development are eventually implemented, the Hampi Authority may wish to draw on the support of UNESCO, which has now added Vijayanagara to its World Heritage List in recognition of the global importance of the site. This international organization has experts experienced in historic conservation and funds, both of which could benefit the site. But Vijayanagara cannot be the sole responsibility of any single authority. It demands the concern of all those who have a direct impact on the site as well as the attention of an international audience. As one of the world's great ruined cities, Vijayanagara evokes the achievements of its rulers, partners of the gods. The City of Victory stirs the imagination of all for whom the power of myth is still alive.

(65) Colonnades of the Hampi bazaar stretching eastward into the rocky landscape of the sacred center.

(66) Lookout post at the summit of the rocky ridge on the north boundary of the urban core.

SITE DESCRIPTIONS

Many hundreds of monuments survive at Vijayanagara's vast site. Some stand relatively complete; others are now merely piles of rubble. Buried foundations of yet other structures continue to be uncovered by archaeologists. This description of Vijayanagara's key monuments focuses on the buildings of greatest historical and artistic importance. The sequence follows the principal spatial divisions of the city: sacred center, irrigated valley, urban core, royal center, and suburban centers (Figures 1 and 3). References to inscriptions are given whenever these provide identifications and dates for buildings. (See bibliography for abbreviations.)

SACRED CENTER

The northern part of the Vijayanagara site is dominated by the Tungabhadra River, which flows in a northeasterly direction through a rocky gorge. Sloping granite shelves and outcrops of boulders, sometimes massed into high hills such as Matanga, offer dramatic views of the river. The riverbank and these hills are the locations of the numerous temples and shrines that constitute the sacred center of the capital (Figure 67). Relief carvings and monolithic sculptures are associated with many of these religious structures.

The sacred center has a longer history than the city itself. Some shrines date back to the eighth and ninth centuries, when the Rashtrakutas dominated the region. Others belong to the period of the Late Chalukyas, in the eleventh and twelfth centuries. Yet other structures date from the fourteenth century, from the decades immediately before and after the foundation of the capital. Most of these pre-Vijayanagara and early Vijayanagara structures are located on or near Hemakuta Hill.

Temple building in the sacred center was particularly active throughout the Vijayanagara era. Many large-scale complexes date from the fifteenth and sixteenth centuries, as do numerous smaller shrines. With the exception of the Virupaksha temple, almost all of the Vijayanagara-period complexes in the sacred center are dedicated to aspects of Vishnu, notably Krishna, Tiruvengalanatha, Narasimha, and Vithala.

Some evidence exists of construction and renovation of the Virupaksha shrines in the seventeenth century, well after the site had been abandoned by the Vijayanagara emperors.

HEMAKUTA HILL (Figures 9, 28, 38, 68-71)
The sacred hill rises south of the village of Hampi, its granite slope dotted with shrines. The hill is encircled on three sides by massive fortifications, creating an irregular quadrilateral. This precinct is bounded on the north by the enclosure wall of the Virupaksha complex and by a colonnade on an elevated terrace, now mostly collapsed.

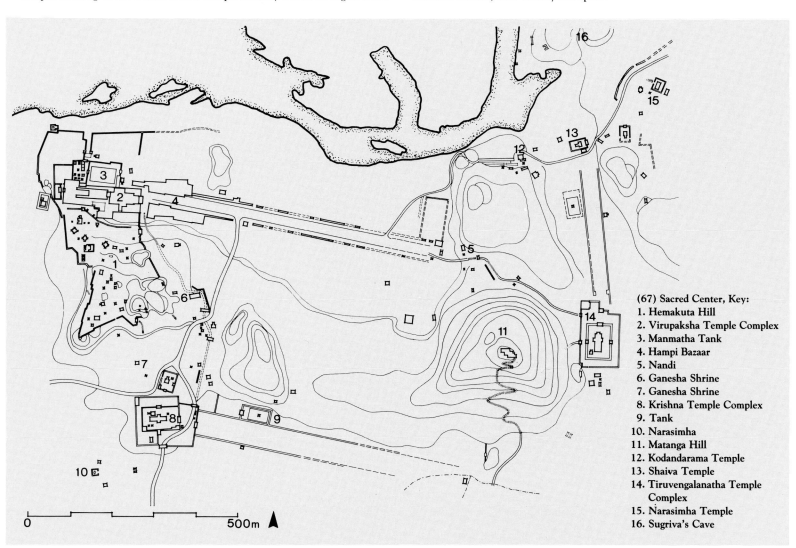

(67) Sacred Center, Key:
1. Hemakuta Hill
2. Virupaksha Temple Complex
3. Manmatha Tank
4. Hampi Bazaar
5. Nandi
6. Ganesha Shrine
7. Ganesha Shrine
8. Krishna Temple Complex
9. Tank
10. Narasimha
11. Matanga Hill
12. Kodandarama Temple
13. Shaiva Temple
14. Tiruvengalanatha Temple Complex
15. Narasimha Temple
16. Sugriva's Cave

0   500m ▲

(68) Hemakuta Hill, Gateway, and Mandapa

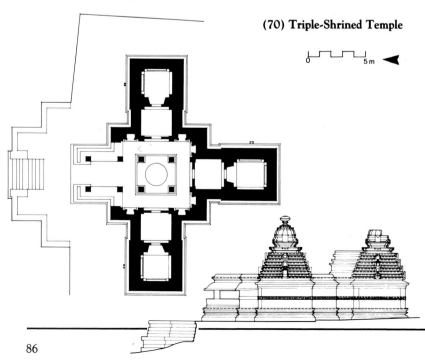

(69) Hemakuta Hill, Triple-Shrined Temples

(70) Triple-Shrined Temple

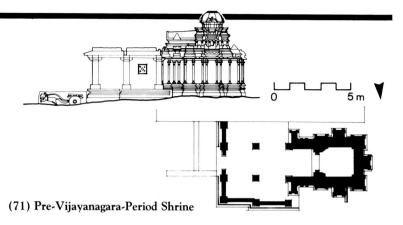

(71) Pre-Vijayanagara-Period Shrine

Hemakuta is commanded by four gateways, two of which consist of open, double-storied colonnades with central walkways at ground level. One gateway is positioned in the colonnade lower down the hill to the north, another is at the summit of the hill to the south. (A third is now blocked up within the Virupaksha complex.) These freestanding structures date to the middle of the fourteenth century immediately after the foundation of the capital, as do the surrounding fortifications. A single-storied gateway with an outer colonnaded porch is set into the walls at the southeast corner of the hill.

Traces of rock-cut steps linking these gateways indicate a path that once led down to the river from the summit of Hemakuta. This south-north route was cut off in the sixteenth century by the enclosure walls of the Virupaksha temple.

An impressive masonry gateway is located near the bottom of the fortifications on the east side. The walls of this structure, which are raised on a molded basement, have repeated shallow pilasters; no tower is preserved above. The gateway may date from the fifteenth century.

Rocky crevices in the hill act as water cisterns. Terraces built at different levels, on which temples and other structures once rested, are indicated by lines of peg holes in the sloping bedrock. These holes anchored granite retaining walls with earthen infilling.

More than thirty shrines stand on Hemakuta Hill. These vary from elaborate structures with multiple sanctuaries to rudimentary, single-celled constructions. Two of the largest temples on the lower slope face north toward the river. These each have three small, square sanctuaries that open off a central columned mandapa, which is extended on the north as a veranda with an overhanging eave. Interiors of these temples are plain except for the columns with double capitals and angled brackets. Exteriors are massive and unadorned, with sharply cut basement moldings, plain walls with horizontal ornamented bands, and simple cornices above. Pyramidal superstructures rising over the sanctuaries are divided into horizontal layers by deeply cut eavelike moldings. Part-circular projections extend from the fronts of the towers; at the summits are domelike roofs with pot finials.

Immediately northwest of these two temples is another, laid out in a similar fashion with sanctuaries on three sides of a central mandapa. The outer walls here have shallow pilasters positioned at regular intervals, dividing the exterior into narrow bays. The towers over the sanctuaries rise in successive and diminishing stories, each marked by a parapet of miniature roof forms. Immediately east of this temple is a small, square shrine with a vaultlike roof.

Though the three triple-shrined temples are almost entirely devoid of carvings, they are all dedicated to Shiva. This is borne out by an inscription in one of the north-facing shrines recording the installation of three lingas by Vira Kampiladeva, a local fourteenth-century chief (ARSIE 1935, no. 353). The epigraph suggests that these three almost identical temples belong to the decades immediately preceding the establishment of Vijayanagara.

One nearby structure may be assigned to a much earlier period. This is a small shrine, built in sandstone rather than in local granite, abutting the north side of a temple with double sanctuaries and plain outer walls. The sandstone shrine has deeply recessed bays and projections marked by pairs of pilasters, above which are the successive stories of the tower. These features are characteristic of ninth- and tenth-century Rashtrakuta architecture.

The modest temples on the upper slope of Hemakuta are generally less finely built; some have been altered by disfiguring additions or partly dismantled. One group consists of three small linga shrines in a row, facing towards open pavilions intended for carved images of Nandi. Further up the hill is the so-called "original" Virupaksha shrine, recognized by its low elevation and pyramidal tower with horizontal moldings. This is probaly the shrine mentioned in two inscriptions dated 1398; these epigraphs are incised on a boulder above a nearby cistern (ARSIE 1935, nos. 351-352). A small structure to the west has recently been converted into a Hanuman shrine.

VIRUPAKSHA TEMPLE COMPLEX (Figures 39, 57, 72-74)

This is the most important temple at Vijayanagara today and the chief place of worship at Hampi. The main object of devotion in the complex is the linga identified with Virupaksha, but there are other deities of importance, such as the goddesses Pampa and Bhuvaneshvari. While the original Virupaksha sanctuary is likely to be a pre-Vijayanagara period structure, its present appearance is mostly due to sixteenth-century construction, when the temple was greatly enlarged under the patronage of Krishnadevaraya.

The complex is laid out in two large enclosures, with a connecting towered gateway aligned along an east-west axis. At the far end of the inner (western) enclosure is the principal temple. The small, square sanctuary at the core of this structure may well belong to the ninth or tenth century, contemporary with other Rashtrakuta-period shrines such as those on Hemakuta Hill and another overlooking Manmatha Tank to the north. It is, however, not possible to observe the architectural features of the original Virupaksha sanctuary, since it is now concealed within later additions, with access restricted to brahmin priests.

The second phase of construction of the complex dates from the fourteenth century, soon after the foundation of the capital. At this time, the Vir-

upaksha sanctuary was enlarged by the provision of walls on three sides and a small antechamber in front (east); the space between these additions and the original structure became a dark, narrow passageway. The architectural character of these extensions is evident in the outer walls of the sanctuary and passageway, partly obscured by later additions and plasterwork. The walls are raised on sharply defined basement moldings, with regularly spaced, shallow pilasters. A superstructure of the pyramidal type, divided into horizontal layers by deeply recessed, eavelike moldings, rises above.

This modest shrine was expanded in the late fifteenth century by the addition of another antechamber, now housing a brass image of Nandi, and an enclosed mandapa with doorways on four sides. An inscription on the mandapa wall appears to refer to Saluva Narasimha, ursurper of the Vijayanagara throne in 1485. The open mandapa with columns and piers arranged around a large central space was added in 1510 during the reign of Krishnadevaraya (ARSIE, 1889, no. 29; EI, I, pp. 361-371).

While the treatment of the columns in the inner mandapa is restrained, the columns and piers of the sixteenth-century mandapa are carved with considerable virtuosity. The piers in the middle of the outer rows and at the corners of the inner hall are sculpted with rearing yalis with lion bodies, elephantlike heads, and elongated snouts. Other piers have two or more fluted colonettes clustered around central shafts carved with diverse mythological figures. The doorway at the western end of this mandapa is flanked by large, four-armed guardian figures.

The outer wall of the earlier, enclosed mandapa consists of a number of bays flanked by pilasters; projecting porches with carved columns lead to doorways on the north and south. The balustrades on either side of the access

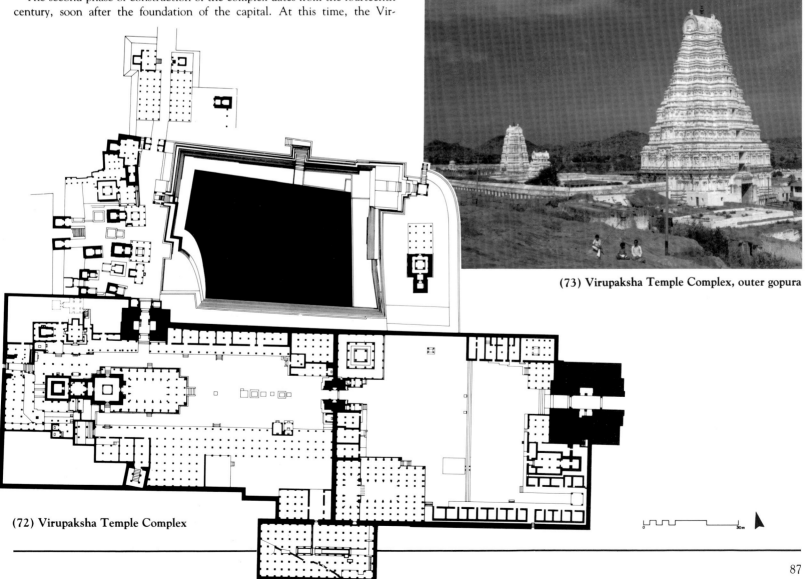

(73) Virupaksha Temple Complex, outer gopura

(72) Virupaksha Temple Complex

(74) Virupaksha Temple Complex, inner court

steps are carved as yalis with sinuous trunks. The outer columns of the open mandapa are sheltered by an overhanging, double-curved eave. The brick and plaster parapet above is divided into niches with cusped arches containing standing images of Shiva and Parvati. Each niche is surmounted by a miniature temple tower. Seated Nandi images are positioned at the corners of the parapet.

Important paintings cover the raised ceiling over the enlarged central space of the outer mandapa. The paintings are no earlier than the eighteenth century and are possibly contemporary with other late additions to the temple. The paintings are divided into panels of different sizes, symmetrically arranged around a central carved lotus medallion. The sinuous black line work on a red background contrasts with the turquoise, green, brown, and white colors. The figures are depicted in animated and varied poses. The faces are generally shown in profile, with prominent eyes and pointed noses.

Almost all of the painted subjects are mythological, but there is an unusual representation of a procession in which the sage Vidyaranya is carried in a palanquin, in the company of soldiers and drummers. The most important panels are arranged in matching pairs: the marriage of Shiva and Parvati is coupled with the marriage of Rama and Sita and the ten incarnations of Vishnu with the regents of the universe's directions (riding their respective animals). Manmatha, god of love, shoots an arrow at Shiva, who sits undisturbed in meditation; Shiva aims arrows at three demons, each shown within a small circle representing a fortress. Modern relief plaster sculptures conceal beams on four sides of the paintings.

Low altars and two wooden posts sheathed in brass with metal lamp holders at the top stand in front (east) of the Virupaksha shrine. The courtyard is surrounded by an elevated colonnade of piers composed of clustered colonettes. This colonnade contains earlier structures. On the north side, steps lead down to a small chamber, once a shrine, at ground level. Two small chambers above are dedicated to Pampa and Bhuvaneshvari, both identified

as Shiva's consorts. The interiors of these goddess shrines are notable for their gray-green schist columns, beams, ceilings, and doorways, all carved in an ornate and highly intricate manner. The use of schist and its delicate treatment are typical features of the twelfth-century Late Chalukya style. Small subsidiary structures on the west and south sides of the court enshrine other deities. The Sarasvati shrine contains a sculpted image, also of the Late Chalukya era. The shrine on the west side of the colonnade devoted to the sage Vidyaranya dates from the early Vijayanagara period.

The inner court of the complex is entered through two towered gopuras. That on the east is a modest structure. The lower, granite portion has basement moldings and walls divided by pilasters, partly concealed on the east by later shrines. The upper, brick tower has two diminishing stories capped by a barrel-vaulted roof. The inscription of 1510 already referred to mentions this gopura, which may have been standing at this time. The gopura on the north side of the court that leads to the shrines overlooking Manmatha Tank is much larger. Its massive lower granite stage, which resembles that of the incomplete gateway on the east slope of Hemakuta Hill, may be assigned to the fifteenth century. The upper portion of this northern tower, however, is quite different in style and probably belongs to the eighteenth century. The soaring tower is a steep pyramid of brick and plaster, divided into ascending and diminishing stories. Pilasters are grouped around the regularly spaced shallow projections, which are devoid of sculptures. The capping roof is of the usual barrel-vaulted type.

By far the most impressive gateway of the complex provides access to the outer enclosure from the east, the direction from which the temple is approached along the colonnaded street. Though there is no foundation date for this immense structure, it is hardly possible that it predates the reign of Krishnadevaraya; certainly it can be no earlier than the additions of 1510 already noted. This is the largest gopura at Vijayanagara, with a vertical rise of more than 50 meters. It is almost square in plan, with pronounced projections on four sides. The granite base is divided into two stories with an intermediate basement molding and deeply recessed niches, now missing their sculptures. The upper brick and plaster tower has eight superimposed and diminishing stories, each with an opening in the middle of the front and back; the capping roof is barrel-vaulted. The interior passageway of the gopura is partly roofed with a pointed arched vault of Islamic inspiration. This departure from the more usual horizontal roof slabs may have been dictated by structural considerations.

The outer (eastern) enclosure of the complex, which is reached after passing through this gopura, is a large, rectangular space lined on four sides with colonnades and minor shrines. Some concrete structures have recently been added. The mandapa at the northwest corner, immediately north of the intermediate gopura, dates to the fifteenth century. In the middle is a raised dais for display of processional images; the surrounding columns have carved blocks on the shafts. At the southwest corner of the court is a spacious, "hundred-columned" kalyana mandapa for the marriage ceremonies of the god and goddess. This structure is elevated on an elaborately carved basement and has an enlarged rectangular space in the middle. The columns are slender, with carved blocks on the shafts, sometimes encircled by clusters of colonettes. Three bays at the western end of the hall are raised on a platform.

A doorway in the south side of the kalyana mandapa leads into the kitchen, which consists of a simple colonnade on four sides of a long narrow court. A water channel is cut into the rocky floor. Other kitchens are located outside the temple to the west of the principal shrine. Here too are meeting halls and residential quarters associated with the Vidyaranya matha, a relatively modern residence for teachers and students. A short distance southwest of this complex is a square tank surrounded by a dilapidated colonnade.

SHRINES OVERLOOKING MANMATHA TANK (Figure 75)

Immediately north of the Virupaksha complex is a large rectangular reservoir with stepped sides known as Manmatha Tank. This is an important bathing place for priests and worshipers. A group of small shrines on the west side of the tank faces east toward the water. These structures line the path leading from the river to the northern gopura of the Virupaksha complex. Before

(75) Manmatha Tank, shrine

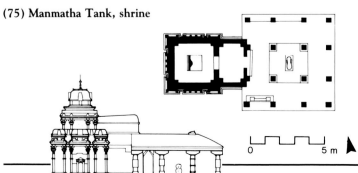

reaching this temple, however, the path passes through two gateways, one of which is an extensive columned structure.

The Manmatha Tank shrines are early in date, comparable with those on Hemakuta Hill, but dilapidated and partly buried in the ground. They consist of single square sanctuaries with pyramidal towers attached to open, columned mandapas with steeply sloping roof slabs.

One shrine of imported sandstone is probably the earliest intact building of the group, belonging to the Rashtrakuta era in the eighth or ninth century. Its exterior walls have pilastered projections and recesses; the central niches are topped by frames with miniature makaras, or aquatic beasts. The diminishing stories of the small, square tower are capped with a domelike roof. The columned mandapa with granite columns in front is an addition of the Vijayanagara period. An inscribed slab within this hall, however, is much earlier, since it records a gift to the god Virupaksha by a local chief in 1199 (ARSIE, 1889, no. 31). A sculpture of a hero killing a lion with a sword is placed near this slab. A large, eight-armed image of Durga is enshrined within the sanctuary.

The adjacent shrine to the south is of a similar design, but here the material is the more readily available granite. This structure may not be as old as the previous example and probably belongs to the Late Chalukya period in the eleventh or twelfth century.

Other structures of this group are all of granite and have familiar pyramidal towers with deeply recessed horizontal tiers of eavelike moldings. Some superstructures are concealed within modern plaster repairs. Many of these shrines can be assigned to the fourteenth century.

A Vijayanagara-period temple is located on a terrace at the east end of the tank. The open colonnade abuts a small, closed hall that leads to a north-facing sanctuary. This structure has recently been cleared and reconstructed; many stone slabs carved with nagas, or snakes, were discovered nearby. A staircase leads from present ground level to a small pavilion north of the temple, from which steps descend to the tank. Other early temples are hidden inside the houses that stand to the east of the tank.

HAMPI BAZAAR (Figures 16, 55, 58, 65, 76)
The ceremonial street for chariot festivals stretching eastward from the principal gopura of the Virupaksha temple serves as the main commercial thoroughfare of the village of Hampi. It is known locally as the Hampi bazaar. The street, more than ten meters wide and almost 750 meters long, was originally lined along its entire length with raised colonnades and structures. At its western end, near the temple entrance, these colonnades and structures are incorporated into newly built shops, tea stalls, and residences; elsewhere, they are occupied by squatters. The colonnades are generally simple structures with crudely fashioned columns, one bay deep. More elaborate structures have two stories, with double-height columns surmounted by parapets on the

(76) Hampi Bazaar, structure

street facade. Balconies at the upper levels suggest that they were intended as platforms from which to view the chariot processions. It is likely that such structures served as temporary residences for courtly visitors at festival time, while the colonnades accommodated merchants and traders. The remains of lesser structures are concealed in fields on either side of the bazaar.

The Hampi bazaar was originally surfaced in stone; recent clearing work at the eastern end of the street has revealed granite pavement blocks. Large mandapas, now reconstructed, were probably rest houses for visiting brahmins. A crudely fashioned granite lamp column stands nearby. At the end of the street, a double-storied structure with chlorite columns faces west toward the temple. The circular shafts and capitals of these columns are Late Chalukya in style and were probably brought from a dismantled building at or near the site. This structure, which marks the furthest point that chariots can be pulled, may have been used for the display of processional images.

A pavilion to the northeast shelters a large rock-cut image of Nandi. A later recutting of the bull's head gives the animal a curiously primitive appearance. Stone steps and pavement slabs indicate a road that led over a hill to the Tiruvengalanatha temple in the adjacent valley. The road passes through a large, open gateway structure.

MONOLITHIC GANESHA IMAGES AND NEARBY GATEWAYS (Figure 57)
A short distance east of the Hemakuta fortifications, near the top of the ridge that joins Hemakuta and Matanga Hills, is a sanctuary with an elegant, colonnaded porch. The porch and an open area in front are supported on a massive retaining wall. The porch columns are unusually slender and tall, with triple sets of blocks carved in the typical sixteenth-century style. The sculpted columns contrast with the unadorned walls of the shrine. The interior is dominated by a large image of Ganesha, more than 4.5 meters high, carved out of a single boulder.

A gateway immediately southeast of this Ganesha shrine is built across the road that originally led down to Hampi and which is indicated by well-worn pavement slabs. The gateway itself consists of an open, columned structure with three passageways wide enough to take wheeled traffic. Stone doorjambs and lintels were for wooden doors, now vanished. Further evidence of the same road exists further south, where there are smaller gateway structures of the same type, as well as pavement slabs and stone steps.

A second but smaller monolithic Ganesha sculpture is located south of Hemakuta Hill. This image is visible from the outside, since the god is seated within an open pavilion.

KRISHNA TEMPLE COMPLEX (Figures 44, 47, 77-80)
This large religious edifice overlooks a valley of irrigated crops. The temple is no longer used for worship, having been badly vandalized at the time of the city's destruction. Many sculptures are disfigured, and the eastern gopura has partly collapsed; recently, the temple has undergone extensive restoration. The complex was built by Krishnadevaraya and was the first large-scale monument to be erected during his reign. It was completed in 1515 to commemorate a victorious military campaign of the Vijayanagara forces (SII, IV, nos. 254-255). The temple once enshrined an image of Balakrishna that, according to the epigraph, was removed from the fort at Udayagiri in the eastern Ghats. (This sculpture, which depicts the god as an infant, is now displayed in the Government Museum in Madras.)

The Krishna temple is contained within a double set of high enclosure walls, one within the other. The inner enclosure is rectangular; the outer enclosure is irregular and is divided by cross walls into two parts. Fish and mythical water beasts are carved in low relief on wall blocks. The modern road linking Kamalapuram to Hampi now proceeds through the eastern half of the outer enclosure, passing directly in front of the eastern gopura. A large gateway with triple passageways interrupts the south side of the outer enclosure and is, therefore, earlier than the enclosure walls that abut it at either end. This freestanding structure resembles a similar gateway on the ridge overlooking Hampi. Another gateway in the north wall of the outer enclosure has been dismantled. The inner enclosure has towered gopuras on the north, east, and south; only the one on the east, is truly monumental in scale.

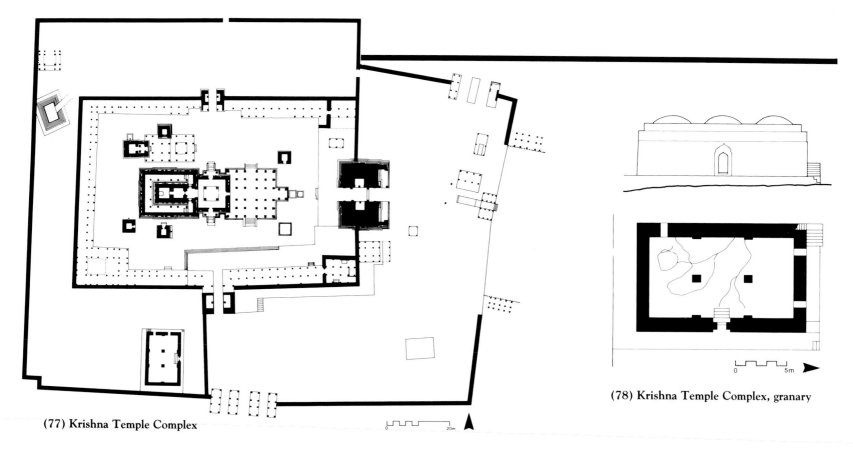

(77) Krishna Temple Complex

(78) Krishna Temple Complex, granary

The temple that stands in the middle of the inner enclosure consists of an outer, open columned mandapa; an inner, enclosed columned mandapa with four doorways (the two on the north and south approached through porches); an antechamber with doorways leading to a dark, narrow circumambulatory passageway; and, at the core of the building, a small, square sanctuary, now empty. The interior of the temple is massive and unadorned except for carved blocks on the column shafts. The exterior has a long, low elevation, with continuous basement moldings. Regularly spaced wall niches are flanked by pilasters, as well as single pilasters standing in pots; diverse images carved in low relief adorn the intermediate surfaces. Over the sanctuary rises a brick and plaster tower, now much eroded. The two square stories are capped by a hemispherical roof. The open mandapa at the eastern end of the temple has monolithic piers with clustered colonettes on the outer rows.

A small pavilion stands immediately in front of this mandapa, abutting the middle of its eastern side and blocking the view of the interior of the temple from the entrance gopura. This pavilion was probably intended to house an image of Garuda, the eagle mount of Vishnu. Other small structures are grouped around the main temple. The simple shrine to the south may have been dedicated to Subrahmanya; that to the northwest, which is approached through a long columned hall and an antechamber, was devoted to Lakshmi. The plaster towers of these smaller structures are newly made, though traditional in style.

An opening beside the blocked gateway in the southern enclosure wall leads to the western half of the outer enclosure, where a granary is built upon a sloping rocky shelf. This rectangular structure is related to the courtly monuments of the royal center. It has an elevation entirely devoid of features except for a small doorway on the east. An external staircase ascends to the roof, where there are six shallow domes, each with a small hole, presumably through which to pour grain. The interior consists of six domed bays.

Though ruined, the rectangular eastern gopura is still impressive. It has high, colonnaded porches on either side of the outer (eastern) doorway; the columns have recently been reset. The rear walls of the porch have the standard arrangement of niches and pilasters. The ruined brick tower, with many plaster sculptures still intact, rises above. On the rear (west) face is a dramatic frieze of warriors with shields, together with horses and elephants, possibly depictions of the troops of Krishnadevarya's army.

A short distance in front (east) of the gopura, on the other side of the modern road, steps descend to the ceremonial chariot street. This was once lined with colonnades but is now planted with sugarcane and banana groves

(79) Krishna Temple Complex, gopura

(80) Krishna Temple Complex, shrine

that partly conceal the dilapidated structures. Extending eastward from the temple, the street is as wide as that of the Virupaksha complex and no less than five hundred meters long. A large reservoir, now empty, was located beyond the east end of the street. On the north side of the street is a large rectangular reservoir. This has stepped sides and is surrounded by a colonnade with an entrance gateway on the west. A small pavilion with a brick and plaster tower stands in the middle of the water.

MONOLITHIC NARASIMHA IMAGE AND LINGA SHRINE (Figure 36)
A short distance south of the Krishna Complex is an imposing sculpture of the Narasimha incarnation of Vishnu. This is hewn out of a single boulder and, at a height of about 6.7 meters, is the largest image at Vijayanagara. According to an associated inscription, the Narasimha was fashioned at the order of Krishnadevaraya in 1528 (ARSIE, 1889, no. 34). The sculpture was badly mutilated, presumably during the sack of Vijayanagara, but is currently undergoing restoration. The fierce, lion-headed god is seated as a yogi in lotus posture with a diminutive figure of his consort, the goddess Lakshmi, positioned on his lap. The shattered pieces of Lakshmi are now being reassembled. Rising over the head of the god is a multiheaded cobra hood surmounted by a yali head with protruding eyes. These form part of an arch supported on two freestanding columns, all cut out of a granite boulder. The monolith stands in an open structure of high walls with an entrance doorway on the east.

Immediately north of Narasimha is a square shrine that contains a large, polished linga almost three meters high. Because of recent irrigation in the vicinity, the interior of the shrine is frequently flooded.

SARASVATI TEMPLE
The temple, which was probably originally dedicated to Krishna, lies to the east of the modern road that connects Hampi with Kamalapuram and near the Turuttu Canal, which runs along the south side of the irrigated valley. Traces of plasterwork, including fully modeled figures and ornamental motifs, suggest the rich decoration that covered the apparently simple structures. The brick parapet has mutilated figures, including a group with Balakrishna. A relief carving on a boulder a short distance to the east depicts a two-armed, seated figure of Sarasvati. The goddess holds a palm-leaf book in her hands.

VAISHNAVA TEMPLE AND VIRABHADRA TEMPLE
A short distance south of the Sarasvati temple the Hampi-Kamalapuram road makes a turn, passing in front of two temples. The first temple faces eastward and has elaborately carved yali columns on the outer columns of the mandapa. This hall provides access to two small shrines. Above the principal shrine rises a brick tower with a hemispherical roof; the pedestal inside has an image of Garuda carved onto its base. A colonnade runs around the two shrines. To the west of this temple is an extensive mandapa, with clerestories, possibly a feeding house for brahmins. The Turuttu Canal flows nearby.

The Virabhadra temple stands within a walled compound, facing north toward a monolithic lamp column beside the modern road. The temple is currently used for worship, the principal object of devotion being a four-armed image of Virabhadra more than three meters high. An inscription records that the temple was founded in 1545 (SII, IV, no. 266).

MATANGA HILL (Figure 7)
The highest point within the Vijayanagara site is named after the sage connected with Pampa and also with Sugriva and Hanuman. Despite these associations, the shrine at the summit of Matanga Hill is actually dedicated to Virabhadra, a fierce form of Shiva. From its roof there is a spectacular panorama of the site, in particular of the Tiruvengalanatha temple and its chariot street immediately beneath the hill to the east. The ascent to Matanga is most easily achieved from the south, where gigantic granite steps lead upward from the irrigated valley. Inscriptions and low-relief carvings on boulders line the route. Steps in considerable disrepair also ascend from south of the bazaar street of the Virupaksha temple and from the Tiruvengalanatha temple.

KODANDARAMA TEMPLE
An important temple dedicated to Kodandarama stands beneath the northern slope of Matanga Hill, overlooking the Tungabhadra at the point where the river turns northward. The temple faces the pilgrims' path that follows the south bank of the river, connecting Hampi with the Vithala complex to the northeast. The path follows the fortifications that defend the river approach to the city. The bathing ghat nearby, known locally as Chakra tirtha, is believed to be the spot where Shiva gave the magical chakra weapon to Vishnu. Long stone steps descend to the river.

The temple has a columned mandapa with tall shafts fashioned with blocks in the typical sixteenth-century manner. The sanctuary is built against a large boulder carved with standing figures of Rama, Sita, and Lakshmana. Several crudely built shrines to the rear of the temple are grouped together on the lower slope of Matanga Hill. They are dedicated to Hanuman and Sudarshana, the latter depicted as a human figure with sixteen hands. Another small temple to the east has a plaster figure of reclining Vishnu on the parapet above the porch.

ROCK-CUT SCULPTURES (Figures 2, 10)
Images are carved in relief on boulders beside the river. The blackened color of these rocks indicates that they were periodically submerged by floodwaters before the completion of the Tungabhadra dam. Nonetheless, the sculptures are well-preserved. They include a fine representation of Vishnu as Anantashayana reclining on the serpent and a double row of Vishnu figures depicting the twenty-four emanations of this god. The presence of Shiva is indicated by two groups of miniature lingas arranged in symmetrical fashion as large, square mandalas with central, enlarged lingas. These compositions are carved on the horizontal surface of the rock and have drainage spouts to carry away libations offered in worship. Another group of rock-cut sculptures, including Nandi, Ganesha, and a linga, is located at the river crossing to Anegondi.

A small, blackened temple built on a rocky shelf on the north side of the river is hidden behind large boulders. It was once approached by a stone causeway, now dismantled by floods.

TIRUVENGALANATHA TEMPLE COMPLEX (Figures 37, 45, 81-82)
The unusual northern orientation of this complex is explained in part by the course of the valley in which the temple and its long ceremonial chariot street are laid out. The valley, which proceeds northward to the river, is bounded by Matanga Hill to the west and Gandhamadhana Hill to the east. The complex is commonly known as Achyutadevaraya's temple, even though the patron is known to have been Hiriya Tirumala, the king's brother-in-law and chief minister. An inscription on the northern gopura records that the temple was consecrated in 1534, when an image of Vishnu as Tiruvengalanatha was installed in the sanctuary (SII, IX, no. 564). The shrine and surrounding structures are currently undergoing reconstruction.

(81) Tiruvengalanatha Temple Complex, mandapa

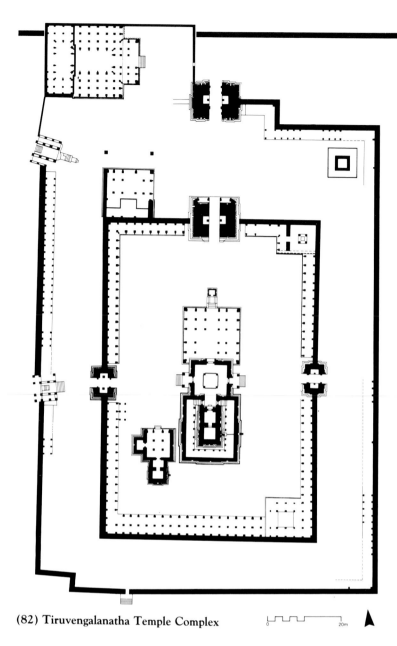

(82) Tiruvengalanatha Temple Complex

Hiriya Tirumala's temple is one of the largest at Vijayanagara and the only one provided with two complete rectangular courts, one within the other, each bounded by high walls. The monumental towered gopuras placed in the north wall of each enclosure constitute the first example of multiple, aligned entrances to a single building. Additional gateways to the inner enclosure are positioned on the east and west; the outer enclosure has an elevated gateway on the west from which a path ascends to Matanga Hill. The small doorway in the south wall leads to a path that runs into the irrigated valley. A small shrine faces on the path, next to which is a boulder carved with a multiarmed image of Kali, now brightly painted.

The central shrine of the Tiruvengalanatha complex occupies the middle of the inner courtyard. At its core are the sanctuary and antechamber, surrounded on three sides by a narrow, unlit circumambulatory passageway. To the north are the enclosed mandapa with doorways on four sides and porches on the east and west and the adjoining large, open mandapa; this is blocked off in the middle of the northern side by a small shrine, probably intended for an image of Garuda. The temple is almost devoid of sculpture, except for carvings on the blocks of column shafts. The sanctuary is empty and its ceiling now missing. Much of the massive ceiling of the outer mandapa has also collapsed. The exterior is similarly plain except for continuous basement moldings and the pilastered walls of the sanctuary and enclosed mandapa. Only the lower portions of the brick and plaster tower over the sanctuary survive. The corner piers of the outer mandapa have colonettes grouped around central shafts; the intermediate piers of the outer row are carved with

fully modeled, rearing yalis. Part of the brick and plaster parapet with recessed niches, now empty, is preserved above the double-curved eave.

A shrine with two sanctuaries, possibly for each of Vishnu's goddesses (Bhudevi and Lakshmi), stands near the southwest corner of the temple. The colonnade that runs around four sides of the inner enclosure is dilapidated, with some columns leaning dangerously. A similar colonnade extending around the inside of the outer enclosure has recently been dismantled to facilitate rebuilding. More highly decorated structures stand in the outer enclosure, including a partly ruined hall west of the inner northern gopura and a more completely preserved hall west of the outer northern gateway. The latter mandapa has fine carvings on the column blocks, including animated figures of gods, sages, and maidens. The raised floor at the rear (west) of the hall may have been for the marriage celebrations of the divinity. The aerial view of this structure from Matanga reveals massive stone beams spanning the central open hall.

The two northern gopuras are impressive structures, even though the outer one is partly ruined. Their rectangular granite bases have high basement moldings and pilastered walls with regularly spaced niches. The incarnations of Vishnu are carved on the blocks that flank the entrances. Above rise the ruined brick and plaster towers. These pyramidal compositions are divided into successive stories, but the plaster sculptures are mostly lost.

A ceremonial street runs northward from the gopura in the outer enclosure. While this street is neither as broad nor as long as those that run eastward from the Virupaksha and Krishna complexes, it nonetheless provides the Tiruvengalanatha temple with an impressive approach from the north. The colonnade on the east side of the street still stands, but that on the west has partly collapsed. Fields irrigated from a nearby water channel now occupy the street itself. Ruins of collapsed rubble structures are visible on the hill to the east of the street. A rectangular stepped tank with a central pavilion and a surrounding colonnade, now overgrown, is situated immediately west of the northern end of the street.

Further north, beside the path that leads along the Tungabhadra bank, stands a shaiva temple. This badly ruined shrine stands within a courtyard entered on the east through a monumental gateway. The treatment of the granite basement moldings and pilastered walls indicates that these are sixteenth-century constructions.

NARASIMHA TEMPLE AND SUGRIVA'S CAVE (Figures 6, 83)

The small Narasimha temple is the earliest structure still standing in this part of the sacred center. According to an inscription incised on a rock within the courtyard, it may be dated to 1379 (VPR, 1984-87, no. 58). The shrine presents an exterior that is plain except for relief carvings of Garuda and Hanuman. Like examples on Hemakuta Hill, the pyramidal tower over the sanctuary has recessed horizontal moldings. The temple stands in a compound

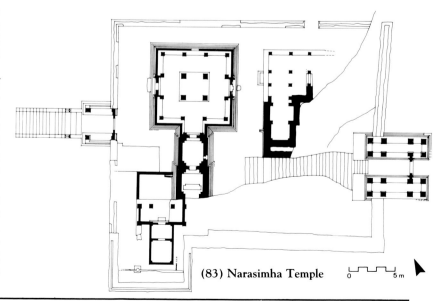

(83) Narasimha Temple

(84) Aqueduct

century. The many inscriptions dating from 1513 until 1554 indicate that substantial additions were made during the reigns of Krishnadevaraya, Achyutadevaraya, and Sadashiva.

The monument, which is dedicated to Vishnu in the form of Vithala, consists of a large, rectangular court bounded on four sides by high walls. The court is entered through three gateways, the most impressive being the gopuras on the east and south. A collapsed colonnade lines the inner face of the enclosure walls. In the middle of the court stands the principal temple. To the northeast is a smaller, secondary shrine, dedicated in 1529 to Vishnu as Adinarayana (according to an inscription on its basement). There are two freestanding columned halls; a third hall is built into the south colonnade. A small shrine fashioned in the form of a ceremonial chariot stands in front (east) of the principal temple.

The main temple consists of a small, square sanctuary and an antechamber surrounded on three sides by a dark, narrow passageway. To the east are an inner, enclosed mandapa with four doorways, those on the north and south leading to porches, and an outer, open mandapa arranged on a stepped plan, with access steps on three sides. The exterior of the passageway and enclosed mandapa presents a long, low facade with uninterrupted basement moldings; pilasters, some of which flank empty niches, are repeated at regular intervals.

bounded by high walls, entered on the west by a flight of steps that leads up from the river. An open, two-storied gateway to the east is similar to those on Hemakuta Hill. From here there is a fine view of the Tungabhadra valley.

Between the Narasimha temple and the river is a mound of high boulders in which there is a deep cleft identified as Sugriva's cave. Ocher and white bands painted on the rocks proclaim the sanctity of the site. A shallow pond nearby, known as Sita sarovar, lies in a rocky depression.

BRIDGE AND AQUEDUCT (Figure 84)

Near these spots is a bridge that once connected the two banks of the Tungabhadra at a point where the river turns eastward. Only the slender granite pylons of the bridge still stand; the walkway, presumably of wood, has now disappeared. A columned mandapa next to the water overlooks the bridge. Recently, this structure has become associated with Purandara Dasa, and it is popular with visitors.

Here, too, may be mentioned the remains of the aqueduct on the northern side of the Tungabhadra, about one kilometer northwest of the ruined bridge. Massive granite pylons support a stone water channel that once transported water to fields.

GATEWAYS AND KING'S BALANCE (Figure 61, 64)

The path that leads along the southern bank of the river toward the Vithala temple partly follows the fortifications that protected this part of the sacred center. The exposed granite sheet rock and buried rubble on either side of the path are littered with small mounds of stone. These have been placed here by pilgrims who believe that this act will ensure fertility and good fortune. The path then passes through an open, two-storied gateway; immediately to the east are several small shrines. Further along is the unusual feature known as the king's balance. This consists of two columns and a lintel, in the middle of which is a stone loop. The metal balance or swing suspended from this loop has long ago vanished.

The path continues toward the southwestern corner of the Vithala temple complex. Before this is reached, however, there stands a large, incomplete gopura. This has fine carvings on the basement and the interior doorway jambs.

VITHALA TEMPLE COMPLEX (Figures 1, 48-51, 85-87)

This is the finest example of religious architecture at Vijayanagara. The temple was vandalized during the sack of the city but has been partly restored to its former splendor. While the original patron and construction date are unknown, the monument is most likely to have been founded in the sixteenth

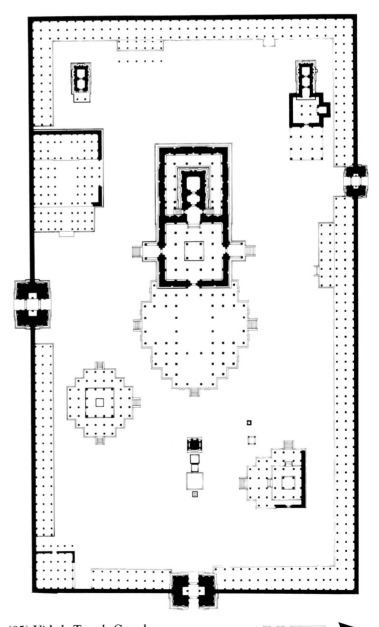

(85) Vithala Temple Complex

(86) Vithala Temple Complex, court

(87) Vithala Temple Complex, mandapa

The brick tower above the sanctuary has a hemispherical roof. The column shafts of the inner mandapa are adorned with carved images. Several of these columns, together with the ceiling slabs that they support, are recent replacements. Large guardian figures flank the broken doorway that leads to the sanctuary. The outer walls of the sanctuary (visible inside the circumambulatory passageway) are more elaborate than those on the exterior of the temple. The moldings of the basement here are delicately carved; single decorated pilasters standing in pots decorate the walls. The interior of the sanctuary is empty except for two empty pedestals for images.

The glory of this temple is the outer, open mandapa, dated 1554 according to an inscription (SII, IX, no. 653). Even though the ceiling is partly destroyed, the monumental conception and elaborately carved architectural elements are still impressive. The mandapa is elevated on an ornate basement and adorned with friezes of elephants and horses with attendants in addition to miniature niches with figures of gods. Carved elephant balustrades flank the access steps. The outer piers have groups of fluted colonettes clustered around central column shafts. (Contrary to popular belief, the tones emitted by these colonettes when lightly struck do not form part of a musical scale.) The lower parts of the piers are carved as miniature lions. The central piers in

the middle of each side are conceived as fully modeled yalis; the beasts are depicted in vigorous rearing postures. The distribution of the inner columns is varied, so as to create open spaces on three sides of a central enlarged hall. Many of these columns are covered with figures and animals, some sculpted almost in the round. The brackets have superimposed corbels supporting heavy roof beams. Where preserved, the beams that span the central hall are more than ten meters long; the ceilings have deeply recessed lotus designs. The outer columns are overhung by a graceful, double-curved eave ornamented with bands of foliation and upraised featherlike motifs at the corners. Stone rings here once supported lamp chains. Only portions of the brick parapet survive.

The small shrine housing an image of Garuda is located immediately east of the main temple. This celebrated structure is designed to imitate a ceremonial temple chariot; accordingly, it is provided with four stone wheels, each ornamented with delicate foliate designs. The wheels are cut out of separate stone blocks and could once be turned on their axles in imitation of the wheels of a true chariot. The sides of this shrine have intricately worked basement moldings with pilastered niches above. Elephant balustrades are positioned beside the entrance steps. The brick superstructure demolished at the end of the nineteenth century, but which appears in the early photographs, consisted of a pyramidal tower capped with a hemispherical roof.

The elegant, freestanding mandapa southeast of the main temple is laid out on a symmetrical plan with double projections on three sides, each reached by a flight of access steps. The outer piers are slender compositions with both clustered colonettes and rearing yalis. Much of the brick parapet over the eave is preserved, especially on the north. The interior columns of the central raised floor area have elaborately sculpted blocks; other interior columns are covered with relief carvings of building facades. The ceiling is an ornate composition with a central lotus.

The mandapa northeast of the main temple is less finely finished; it too has yali carvings on the outer piers. The hundred-columned hall that abuts the southern enclosure wall, southwest of the main temple, is inscribed that it was built by Krishnadevaraya in 1516 (SII, IX, no. 502; XVI, no. 56). Like similar halls in the Virupaksha, Tiruvengalanatha, and Raghunatha complexes, it has an open space in the middle and a raised floor area at the rear (west).

Of the three rectangular gopuras, that in the middle of the south enclosure wall is the best preserved. It follows the standard scheme, with granite walls elevated on a molded basement. Sculpted doorjambs are located in the middle of the passage. The pyramidal tower of brick is divided into stories; almost nothing of the vaulted roof has survived. The gopura on the east is of the same design, but the tower is even more dilapidated. The gateways have inscriptions dated 1538 and 1539 (SII, IV, nos. 256-257; SII, IX, nos. 586, 589). The columned mandapa immediately south of the east gateway, outside the enclosure walls, has collapsed. It has recently been dismantled pending reconstruction. A monolithic lamp column more than twelve meters high once stood in front of the gopura. Only the stump is now visible; the remainder of the shaft lies broken on the ground.

Several shrines stand outside the enclosure walls of the Vithala complex. That to the northeast, dedicated to one of the Vaishnava saints, has an inscription stating that it was erected in 1556, during Sadashiva's reign (SII, IV, no. 279). The temple is a simple structure with an enclosed mandapa, entered through two porches on the north and south and a doorway on the east. The interior has an elaborately carved lotus ceiling. The shrine to the south of the Vithala complex has recently been renovated. An image of a Vaishnava saint installed here is now worshipped as Purandara Dasa.

Two colonnaded streets begin in front (east) of the Vithala complex. The street proceeding northward leads to a walled compound. Inside stands a south-facing temple with three entrance porches. This complex was probably dedicated to one of the Vaishnava saints, such as Ramanuja. Ramayana carvings adorn the walls of the south gateway.

To the southeast is a triple-shrined temple surrounded on four sides by an extensive colonnade. An inscription on one of the columns states that part of the colonnade served as a dining room for brahmins (SII, IX, no. 607).

The street extending eastward from the complex continues for more than five hundred meters; its colonnades, however, are only partly standing. An elaborately decorated mandapa, with a central raised floor area and a small brick tower, is situated just over one kilometer away. This marks the halting place of the ceremonial chariots that were pulled along the street. Halfway down the street on its northern side is a large rectangular reservoir with stepped sides and a domed pavilion in the middle. The water is approached through a gateway in the colonnade to the south. The columns flanking the entrance are carved with horses and riders. Similarly carved columns adorn the mandapa of a shrine diagonally opposite.

IRRIGATED VALLEY

A long valley, running southwest-northeast between parallel rocky ridges south of the sacred center, has an irrigation system that partly dates from the Vijayanagara period. The absence of earthenware ceramics reflects the original uninhabited character of the valley floor. Despite the fact that the Krishna and Tiruvengalanatha complexes of the sacred center intrude into the irrigated valley, there are few structures in this zone; an exception is the U-shaped pavilion. A few small shrines, now covered with vegetation, are built beside canals. Others are located on the hills above the valley (Figures 29 and 31). Well-worn paths, water-storage tanks, mortars for grinding grain, and pottery indicate one-time habitation on the south ridge.

Hydraulic Features
Channels are raised above the valley floor on either side, where they are cut into rocks or supported on stone-lined banks. The Turutta Canal, along the south periphery of the valley, preserves its original Vijayanagara-period name. A natural stream flows northeastward through the middle of the valley toward the Tingabhadra.

A massive, stone-faced dam extended across the valley at its narrowest point, south of Matanga Hill. The walls have been badly eroded, and its central section has disappeared. This dam created a reservoir to the west as well as carrying a road that linked the urban core with the sacred center. At the northern end of this wall, near the foot of Matanga, is a stone bridge across four channels that regulated the flow of water. On the eroded southern end of the wall is a small, collapsing temple next to a stone-paved ramp. Further south, a stone bridge crosses the reconstructed Turutta Canal. Below the dam is a large, columned mandapa with interior shrines. A boulder inside this structure has an inscription that names the dam (VPR, 1983-84, no. 43). A massive structure nearby, now dilapidated and overgrown, may have been part of the water-distribution system.

U-Shaped Pavilion (Figure 63)
This courtly structure, obscured by fields of sugarcane, stands in the middle of the irrigated valley. The building has a number of domed bays arranged in a U-shaped formation open to the east. A balcony once projected outwards from the middle of the west side. Above the arched openings are corbels supporting an angled eave, now fallen. The interior preserves much of its original plasterwork, particularly in the domes and vaults. Remains of water channels are visible nearby.

URBAN CORE

South of the irrigated valley is the urban core of Vijayanagara, notable for its massive fortifications, roads, gateways, and many civic and religious buildings. Numerous temples and shrines are built on granite shelves and against boulders; lookout towers are perched on the summits of rocky outcrops. The largest sacred monument is located on Malyavanta Hill, at the eastern end of the urban core. The northeast, east, and southeast valleys of the urban core are filled with soil from collapsed earth and rubble structures. Numerous buried temples and ruined mandapas, tanks, and wells, together with abundant pottery shards, suggest the dense habitation of this zone during Vijayanagara times.

Evidence of residential areas is more obvious on the bare ridges of the surrounding hills, where there are columned mandapas, temples, shrines, tanks, roads, and, significantly, rubble remains of habitations and pottery fragments. It is possible to associate some areas of the urban core with different social groups. Shrines concentrated in the east valley belong to a Jain quarter; Islamic tombs, cemeteries, and mosques in the northeast valley indicate Muslim residents.

Segments of a dam wall are visible in the southeast of the urban core. (The area contained by these walls is now partly occupied by a water basin of the modern hydroelectric plant.) Elsewhere, tanks, wells, aqueducts, and drains provide abundant evidence of an elaborate hydraulic system. The southwest end of the urban core is occupied by the royal center (see below).

Many roads of the urban core form part of a radial system converging on the royal center (Figure 30). The longest and most important arteries lead along the middle of the northeast, east, and southeast valleys of the urban core; lesser roads proceed north and south. Routes connect the urban core to Hampi and Matanga Hill in the sacred center, to the river crossing to Anegondi to the northeast, and to Kamalapuram to the south.

Balakrishna Temple (Figure 88)
This relatively large and well-preserved temple stands beside the northeast road connecting the royal center with the Islamic quarter. Surrounded by rubble and earth enclosure walls, the temple has recently been cleared to

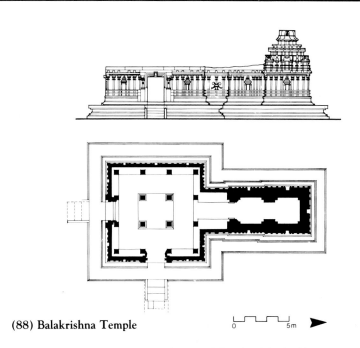

(88) Balakrishna Temple

reveal its stone plinth. The crisply carved details of the building suggest a late fourteenth-century date.

The core of the temple consists of a square, enclosed mandapa with raised seating on four sides, entered through doorways on the east and south. A long antechamber leads to the sanctuary on the north. The outer walls have a basement with sharply cut moldings; regularly positioned, deep niches, now empty, alternate with pilasters, some standing in pots. Over the sanctuary rises the stone tower, in two diminishing stories, with a capping domelike roof. A miniature figure of Balakrishna is carved on the lintel of the eastern doorway.

(89) Mosque

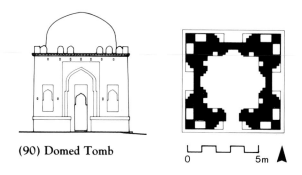

(90) Domed Tomb

MOSQUES AND TOMBS (Figures 89-90)

The Islamic quarter occupies an area that extends from the northern slope of Malyavanta Hill to the fortified ridge that marks the northern boundary of the urban core. Here stand two mosques, a number of tombs both domed and flat-roofed, and clusters of gravestones. Columned structures in this zone, some of which are quite spacious, may have served as rest houses or places of education for the city's Muslim community.

Due to recent reconstruction, only one of the two mosques now stands complete. This mosque consists of a columned hall facing east on an open court. A mihrab niche, headed by a cusped arch cut into the slab, is recessed into the rear (west) wall. The columns have projecting capitals and brackets; the roof is flat. An inscription on a beam, referring to the mosque as a "dhar-mashala," states that it was erected in 1439 by Ahmad Khan (SII, IX, no. 447). Large earthenware pots for water are sunk into the plastered floor of the court. A deep well reached by steps is located a short distance to the north.

A domed tomb stands immediately to the south of the mosque and is ax-ially aligned with it. It is possible that this monument was also built by Ahmad Khan and that it is contemporary with the mosque. The tomb is a small, square structure, with arched recesses in the middle of each side. A parapet of merlons crowns the walls; a dome rises above on a circular drum. Nothing is preserved of this building's original plasterwork. Two other domed tombs in the vicinity are similar, though smaller, with traces of original elaborate plaster ornamentation.

The remainder of the tombs in the Islamic quarter have flat roofs. These small structures are generally built with columns, beams, and infilling walls. The exteriors have arched recesses, parapets of merlons, and, occasionally, parapets with arched openings and corner finials. An inscribed slab near one tomb mentions a Muslim cavalry officer.

GATEWAY ON NORTHEAST AND SOUTHEAST ROADS (Figure 26)

The gate on the northeast road, which leads to Talarighat (the river crossing for Anegondi), has an upper chamber with part of the facade still intact. This

facade has pointed, arched openings with a parapet of merlons. A similarly designed chamber was probably built over a gateway in the southeastern walls of the urban core, but this has mostly fallen. This structure, which is set in a rocky pass, is identified by an inscription as the "hunters' gate" (VPR, 1990). A temple dedicated to Hanuman in the forecourt has an elaborate brick and plaster parapet above the mandala. The temple is aligned with a monolithic lamp column. An extensive enclosure protects entry from the southeast.

RAGHUNATHA TEMPLE COMPLEX (Figures 42, 91-93)

This complex is located on the level summit of Malyavanta Hill, where it is partly concealed by granite boulders. While no historical records are preserved, the architectural style indicates a sixteenth-century date. The temple is situated within a square courtyard bounded by high walls. Aquatic emblems, such as serpents, fish, tortoises, and imaginary monsters, are carved in low relief on the wall blocks. Towered gateways are positioned on the east and south, and there are doorways on the north and west. In the middle of the courtyard is the main temple and, immediately northwest, a smaller shrine with two sanctuaries. A large, columned mandapa abuts the enclosure walls on the south side of the courtyard; nearby is a cistern in a rocky cleft. Subsidiary structures are positioned at the two eastern corners. Immediately in front of the temple is a stone lamp column; the concrete memorial is a modern addition.

The temple contains a large boulder, which forms the west wall of the sanctuary. The natural rock is carved on its eastern face with images of a seated Rama and Sita accompanied by Hanuman and Lakshmana; it is surrounded on three sides by a passageway. Two mandapas extend to the east. The inner hall has four doorways, two of which lead to porches on the north and south; the outer hall is open on three sides.

The exterior walls of the passageway and inner mandapa are relieved only by continuous basement moldings. The parapet is a modern addition. The boulder within the sanctuary protrudes above the roof, where it is capped by a small brick tower with a hemispherical roof, now much restored. The peripheral piers of the open mandapa have colonettes clustered around a central shaft or are fashioned as rearing yalis. An overhanging, double-curved eave shelters the outer columns. The steps are sculpted with elephant balustrades.

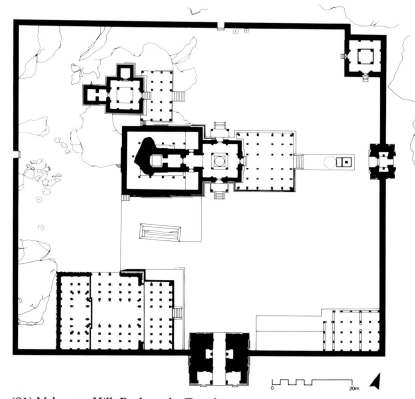

(91) Malyvanta Hill, Raghunatha Temple

(92) Raghunatha Temple, gopura

(93) Raghunatha Temple, shrine

The minor shrine has two sanctuaries opening off a common hall approached through an open mandapa. The exterior is unadorned except for the brick parapet with plaster figures in elaborately decorated niches. Two female images, possibly dating from the Vijayanagara era, are located in the western shrine. The wooden sculpture of Hanuman in the northern shrine, however, is more recent. Both shrines have low, multistoried brick towers capped with vaulted roofs with arched ends; the plasterwork here is ornate. A similarly elaborate brick parapet is preserved on the small structure in the northeast corner of the complex.

The elegant mandapa on the south side of the courtyard is a large structure with finely finished columns fashioned as piers with clustered colonettes. The basement is carved with friezes of courtly animals and attendants. The interior floor, following the rise in ground level, is divided into three ascending levels. The highest level, at the rear (west), is raised on a decorated basement. Pierced stone screens are placed in the north walls.

Immediately in front (south) of the mandapa is the gopura, which dominates the whole complex. This impressive structure is approached on the south side through a deep porch, the columns of which are carved as fully

modeled, rearing yalis. The high basement consists of horizontal bands of delicately carved moldings occasionally interrupted by small templelike niches with carved figures. The porch is overhung by a double-curved eave. Above rise the five diminishing stories of the steeply pyramidal brick tower; these are elaborately treated with pilasters and parapet elements, which are partly concealed by plaster figures. There is a projection in the middle of each side, with guardian figures flanking the openings. The capping, barrel-vaulted roof has arched ends decorated with monster masks. Potlike finials are positioned on the curved ridge of the roof. The rectangular eastern gopura is similar, but smaller in scale and more modest in decoration. There is no porch here.

A doorway in the western enclosure wall of the complex leads to a rocky shelf with a commanding view of the eastern and northeastern valleys of the urban core. A crevice here is lined with rows of small, low-relief Nandi images and Shiva lingas, with drainage spouts to receive libations for worship. A small shrine nearby is fitted into a cavity beneath an overhanging boulder; the Shiva linga inside is cut into the rocky floor of the shrine. A small tower is built on the summit of the boulder (Figure 35).

GANAGITTI JAIN TEMPLE (Figures 41, 94)
This temple is one of the earliest dated monuments at Vijayanagara. According to an inscription on the base of the nearby stone lamp column, it was erected by a minister of Harihara II in 1385 (SII, I, no. 152). The building faces north toward the modern road linking Kamalapuram with the river crossing to Anegondi.

The temple has two connected columned mandapas, each with an adjoining square sanctuary. Porches shelter entrances on the north and east. The

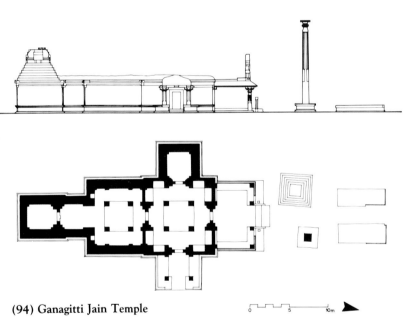

(94) Ganagitti Jain Temple

interior is massive and unadorned except for the columns, which have enlarged capitals, and the decorated doorways. The exterior is similarly plain. The stone tower over the southern sanctuary, which has a stepped pyramidal profile, was once covered with plaster. The brick parapet with plaster figures on the roof of the north porch, now damaged, is a sixteenth-century addition. Immediately in front of the temple are the remains of a gateway and the stone lamp column already referred to.

BHIMA'S GATEWAY (Figure 24)
Immediately southeast of the Ganagitti Jain temple, on one branch of the southeastern road, is the impressive entry complex known as Bhima's gateway. This takes its name from a depiction of the hero Bhima carved on a wall slab. The outer enclosure has a central barbican wall that creates three changes of direction before the gateway itself is reached. The passageway is roofed by slabs supported on triple sets of carved corbels.

(95) Domed Gateway

(96) Gateway on Southwest Road

GATEWAY ON SOUTHWEST ROAD AND HANUMAN TEMPLE (Figure 96)

The gateway on the southwest road is similar to Bhima's gateway, with barbican walls defining a large forecourt. The structure enclosing the passageway is better preserved, however; here, too, multiple brackets are used. A monolithic column and a small, dated Hanuman temple stand facing toward the gateway outside the outer entry of the forecourt.

The temple is of interest because an inscription beside the interior doorway mentions the mid-fifteenth-century ruler Mallikarjuna. The relief carving of the king beneath this epigraph is a rare instance of an identifiable royal portrait. The shrine is a simple structure with a small sanctuary projecting from a partly open, columned hall. The outer walls are plain, and there are traces of a brick tower above. The large image of Hanuman in the sanctuary may have replaced an earlier image of Krishna.

DOMED GATEWAY (Figure 95)

The gateway on another branch of the southeastern road, near the Pattabhirama temple complex outside Kamalapuram, has a well-preserved, outer, square enclosure. Above the outer entry to this enclosure rises a large dome on a circular drum supported on four pointed arches. The dome is constructed of masonry and mortar covered with plaster, in marked contrast with the dry stonework of the enclosure walls beneath. Traces of intricate decoration are preserved in the surviving plasterwork. A ninteenth-century photograph indicates that masonry arches abutted the dome at either side.

ROYAL CENTER

The headquarters of the Vijayanagara kings are located at the western end of the urban core and separated from it by massive walls with gateways on the east, south, and southwest; a line of lesser walls is visible on the north. These fortifications enclose an approximately oval area of about 1.5 kilometers east-west.

Much of the royal center is divided by high walls into irregular and interlocking enclosures. These enclosures are further subdivided into smaller courts and building complexes (Figure 97). The Ramachandra temple stands at the center of these enclosures. Before this temple is the open area where many radial roads converge from the surrounding urban core. Enclosures west of the Ramachandra temple are connected with the king's household and are here designated as the zone of royal residence. Enclosures east of the Ramachandra temple are connected with the public and ceremonial life of the king, referred to here as the zone of royal performance. The boundary between these private and public zones is marked by a north-south alley that leads to the doorway in the south enclosure wall of the Ramachandra temple. The boundary continues to the north of the temple, where there are traces of another north-south alley. This marks the beginning of a road running north toward Matanga Hill.

The eastern portion of the royal center does not appear to be divided into enclosures. This area is dominated by a major road that proceeds in a northeast direction toward the massive gateway in the eastern boundary. Though the road is buried beneath accumulated earth, its presence is clearly indicated by the northwest and southeast alignments of shrines and temples lining its route. Among the features to the south of this road are a temple complex, an octagonal bath, an unexcavated palace, and a rock-cut shrine.

RAMACHANDRA TEMPLE COMPLEX (Figures 11-12, 18, 21, 40, 98-100)

This complex is contained within a rectangle of walls, entered on the east and north through modest gateways, with porches both inside and outside. A small entry on the south side of the enclosure provides access to a north-south alley. The outer face of the enclosure walls on the east, north, and west sides is covered with friezes of courtly subjects. These are divided into four bands, which depict (from bottom to top) parades of elephants, horses being led by attendants, soldiers in martial displays, and dancing women and musicians. Part-circular merlons ornament the tops of the walls. The inner face of the enclosure walls is also partly covered with carvings (north and east sides). These are divided into panels, coinciding with individual blocks, that depict episodes of the Ramayana story. The panels proceed in succesive rows from the northern gateway to the eastern gateway (bottom to top).

A major Rama temple, a smaller, minor temple with two sanctuaries, and several columned halls and pavilions stand within the compound. The major shrine dates from the period of Devaraya I (ruled 1406-22), whose name is inscribed on the basement moldings that flank the main (east) entrance to the columned mandapa (SII, IV, no. 252). An adjacent inscription, datable to 1416-17, records a donation of golden items, possibly by one of Devaraya's queens (SII, IV, no. 251).

The Rama temple consists of a small square sanctuary, an antechamber, and an enclosed, square, columned hall with porches on three sides. The open porch to the east is a sixteenth-century addition. The interior is massive and plain except for the treatment of the mandapa columns: the shafts are elaborately sculpted with images of Vishnu in various incarnations and aspects. The pedestal in the sanctuary is empty.

In contrast, the exterior of the temple is elaborately finished. The basement moldings are intricately carved; the upper moldings include mythical beasts. The outer walls are divided by pilasters that define niches, now empty, on three sides of the sanctuary. The reliefs that cover the wall areas between the pilasters are mostly devoted to illustrating the Ramayana epic. The story is divided into separate panels arranged in three rows (bottom to top); these proceed in a clockwise direction around the mandapa walls, starting on the north wall and ending on the south. A brick tower, now somewhat restored, rises over the sanctuary. It is divided into successive stories, each with pilastered walls, with a capping, domelike roof. The projection on the front (east) face of the tower is arched. Traces of the original plaster figures survive on the lower parts of the tower. The porches leading into the mandapa have finely finished capitals and brackets as well as carvings on the shafts. Deeply curved eaves shelter these columns. The porch extension to the east has elongated columns, each with three blocks of carved images. The brick parapet that rises above the eave is divided into deep niches with plaster figures of Rama and other divinities; templelike towered structures are positioned above.

The minor temple has two sanctuaries opening off a small hall; the porch to the east is a later addition. The elevation of this structure resembles that of the major temple, though here the carving is finer and on a smaller scale. Additional friezes depicting Krishna and other gods are positioned on the basement moldings. Reliefs on the outer walls, between the pilasters, illustrate the conclusion of the Ramayana narrative begun on the main shrine. Sculptures on the east wall depict stories about Narasimha. Brick towers with rectangular vaulted roofs rise over each of the two sanctuaries. The outer walls of the mandapa are plain.

In the northwest corner of the complex is a columned hall bearing an

(98) Ramachandra Temple Complex

inscription 1513, in the era of Krishnadevaraya (SII, IV, no 253). That this is a later addition is indicated by the crude abutment of this structure with Ramayana reliefs carved on the enclosure walls. The open pavilion in the southwest corner of the compound has a raised dais. The colonnades on the west and south sides of the enclosure are crudely built.

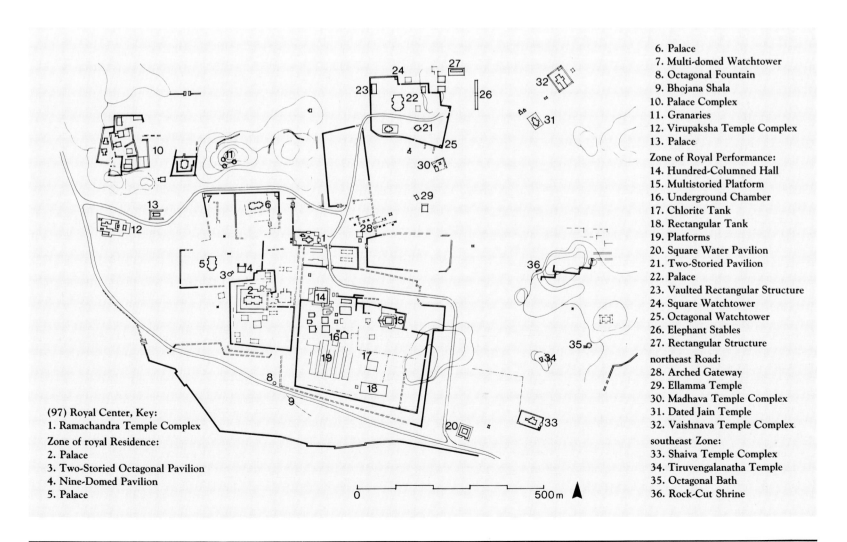

(97) Royal Center, Key:

1. Ramachandra Temple Complex

Zone of royal Residence:

2. Palace
3. Two-Storied Octagonal Pavilion
4. Nine-Domed Pavilion
5. Palace
6. Palace
7. Multi-domed Watchtower
8. Octagonal Fountain
9. Bhojana Shala
10. Palace Complex
11. Granaries
12. Virupaksha Temple Complex
13. Palace

Zone of Royal Performance:

14. Hundred-Columned Hall
15. Multistoried Platform
16. Underground Chamber
17. Chlorite Tank
18. Rectangular Tank
19. Platforms
20. Square Water Pavilion
21. Two-Storied Pavilion
22. Palace
23. Vaulted Rectangular Structure
24. Square Watchtower
25. Octagonal Watchtower
26. Elephant Stables
27. Rectangular Structure

northeast Road:

28. Arched Gateway
29. Ellamma Temple
30. Madhava Temple Complex
31. Dated Jain Temple
32. Vaishnava Temple Complex

southeast Zone:

33. Shaiva Temple Complex
34. Tiruvengalanatha Temple
35. Octagonal Bath
36. Rock-Cut Shrine

0   500 m

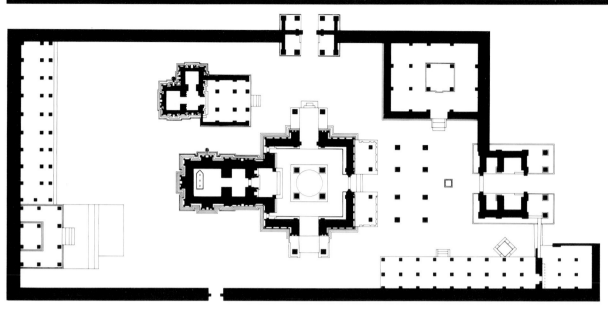

(99) Ramachandra Temple Complex

(100) Ramachandra Temple Complex, shrine

More than eighty meters east of the Ramachandra complex are the remains of a lofty stone lamp column, the shattered parts of which lie scattered. This column was once aligned with the east gateway of the temple complex. Further east is a small shrine probably intended to house an image of Garuda or Hanuman, now much dilapidated. This shrine consists of a small sanctuary adjoining an open porch. A deep, square reservoir surrounded by backrests, and with steps on four sides, is located immediately to the north. Its walls are carved with fish in low relief.

ZONE OF ROYAL RESIDENCE

This zone is divided into enclosures once containing rubble and earth that concealed buried structures. Many of these mounds have been cleared by the Archaeological Survey of India and the Government of Karnataka Department of Archaeology and Museums to reveal masonry basements of palace structures. Excavations in the enclosures northwest of the Ramachandra temple have exposed a densely built-up residential area labeled as the noblemen's quarter by the archaeologists. The nearby temple dedicated to Virupaksha, the same deity worshiped at Hampi, may have been reserved for the king's household.

Several courtly structures still stand in the zone of royal residence. The main examples are a two-storied, octagonal pavilion, a nine-domed pavilion, and a multidomed watchtower. The remains of masonry basements indicate that both palaces and courtly structures were surrounded by colonnades. Elaborate entryways provided access to these diverse structures. These en-

tryways had passageways at ground level flanked by basement moldings. Multiple changes of direction with sequences of gateways ensured privacy and security. Only the masonry foundations of entryways and gateways survive.

PALACES

Royal residences are indicated by stone basements, steps, balustrades, plastered concrete floors, and internal walls of earth and rubble. That timber was also used is indicated by stone footing blocks that once supported columns and the fragments of burned woodwork and metal nails and braces found in the excavations. Fragments of finely wrought plaster sculptures of floral, animal, and human figures are sometimes uncovered in the ruins. Broken earthenware ceramics and Chinese porcelain, stone mortars with which to grind grain, water channels, and even bathing places and latrines suggest the residential function of these structures.

The palaces face either east or north and are laid out on rectangular plans, generally with symmetrically arranged projections with peripheral colonnades. Entry is through a covered court leading to a sequence of two or more ascending levels. Each change in level is defined by basement moldings, often in U-shaped formation, linked by small steps. In the larger examples, the central room on the uppermost level is surrounded by a corridor and two or more small chambers. The remains of steps in some palaces indicate access to a higher level. Larger palaces stand in the middle of open courts and are approached through a complex sequence of gateways and minor courts.

PALACES IN THE SOUTHWEST ENCLOSURES (Figures 101-102)

One of the best-preserved palace structures stands in the middle of the enclosure immediately southwest of the Ramachandra complex. The rectangular plan of this palace has projections on the south, west, and north. The sequence of five ascending levels creates a transition from the court, surrounded on three sides by basement moldings, to the upper square chamber, surrounded by five smaller chambers. Niches in the walls were once filled with figures, but whether these represented humans or gods cannot be determined, since only the lower limbs of the plaster sculptures remain. The palace has subsidiary structures on three sides. In the northeast corner is a complex entryway with minor courts, a finely finished stone water trough, and accessory structures. Stone blocks of the nearby enclosure walls have carvings of gods and one figure with a courtly cap.

Immediately to the south of this palace, within the same enclosure, are the remains of three smaller palaces facing each other from the east, south, and west. These are laid out on rectangular plans with entries at lower levels. Here, however, a cross wall separates the entry and exterior court from an interior court where two pairs of rooms are located to either side of the central chamber.

(101) Palace in Southwestern Enclosure

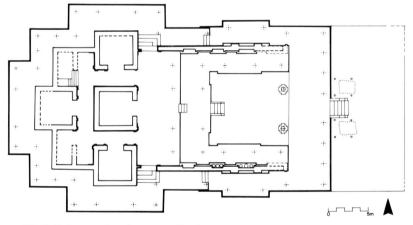

(102) Palace in Southwestern Enclosure

TWO-STORIED OCTAGONAL PAVILION (Figures 34, 103)

This courtly structure stands in the middle of one of the enclosures southwest of the Ramachandra complex, between a large, north-facing palace structure and the nine-domed pavilion. The octagonal building has two domed chambers, one above the other, connected by steps contained within a separate tower. The stone basement, which is square in plan, is extended to accommodate the staircase tower. The exterior preserves much of its original plasterwork, including bands of different designs beneath openings and above arches and brackets with foliate and bird motifs. The circular tower has a ribbed finial.

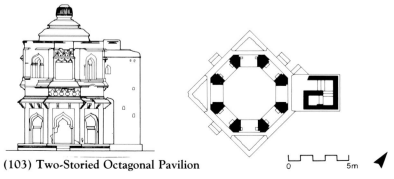

(103) Two-Storied Octagonal Pavilion

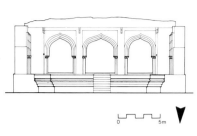
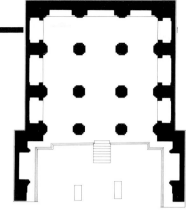

(104) Nine-Domed Pavilion

NINE-DOMED PAVILION (Figure 104)

This pavilion has nine domed bays, with additional recesses on the east, south, and west. The building is open on the north, where walls extend on either side partly to enclose a court (probably once covered). The exterior is now severely plain; a brick parapet has almost disappeared, and only stone brackets suggest a vanished eave. The interior is also unadorned, except for pointed arches and shallow domes. Portions of the basement have moldings with carved friezes, which appear to belong to an earlier palace structure.

A short distance north of the pavilion is a small, square gatehouse roofed with a pyramidal vault.

MULTIDOMED WATCHTOWER (Figure 105)

This structure is built into the northwest corner of one of the enclosures directly west of the Ramachandra complex. The watchtower is raised up on the enclosur's walls and is reached by a long flight of steps. At the upper level there are four domed chambers, those on the west and north having projecting balconies supported on corbeled brackets. The walls and inner surfaces are unadorned.

(105) Multidomed Watchtower

OCTAGONAL FOUNTAIN (Figure 106)

This small building stands beside the modern Kamalapuram-Hampi road in the southwest corner of the zone of royal residence. The structure is laid out on an irregular octagonal plan, with a central domed chamber surrounded by a vaulted arcade. The exterior is plain except for parts of a parapet and a low circular tower. Terra-cotta pipes once conveyed water to the shallow basin in the central chamber from a small tank with sluice gates nearby.

To the north of the fountain, a rectangular courtly building with domed chambers, recorded in a nineteenth-century photograph, has entirely collapsed.

On the other side of the modern road from the octagonal fountain is a water channel more than twenty meters long, flanked by horizontal chlorite

(107) Virupaksha Temple Complex, gopura

(108) Virupaksha Temple Complex, interior

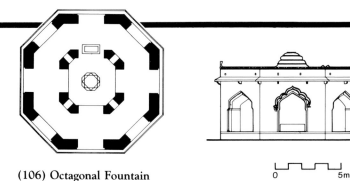

(106) Octagonal Fountain

slabs. These are carved with circular depressions that may have served as dishes. The structure is known as the bhojana shala, or eating hall.

VIRUPAKSHA TEMPLE COMPLEX (Figures 107-109)

This complex is located in the vicinity of the palaces in the western part of the zone of royal residence. It was for some time buried beneath accumulated earth, which is why it is known as the underground temple. The complex has been cleared to reveal a labyrinth of colonnades, minor shrines, and gateways.

The original Virupaksha shrine is a small, east-facing linga sanctuary dating back to the fourteenth century. It is approached through an antechamber and an adjoining columned mandapa once open on three sides. Little is visible other than portions of basement moldings and the tower over the sanctuary. The mandapa columns have cubic shafts and double brackets. The temple was extended throughout the fifteenth century. The first additions were a passageway around the original sanctuary and a second enclosed mandapa in front (east). Colonnades were then built on three sides, as well as a gateway and a monolithic lamp column to the east.

The larger gateway a short distance east of the complex was probably erected toward the end of the fifteenth century. Only the granite lower portions of this structure are present; these have basement moldings and walls with shallow pilasters.

The complex was enclosed in a rectangle of walls during the sixteenth century. At that time, too, a columned hall was erected outside the enclosure to the south. This mandapa, which opens to the east, has an elaborate interior with finely carved basement moldings and columns. An inscribed slab set up inside the hall records a grant by Krishnadevaraya on the occasion of a solar eclipse in 1513 (SII, IX, no. 491).

PALACES IN THE NORTHWEST ENCLOSURES (Figure 67)

The palace structures exposed in the far northwestern part of this zone are set within enclosure walls. Some of their plans are elaborate. One large, north-facing example has a rectangular upper chamber surrounded by three smaller chambers. There is provision for bathing in the southeast corner; a deep well and cistern are positioned nearby. The central chamber of a second palace in

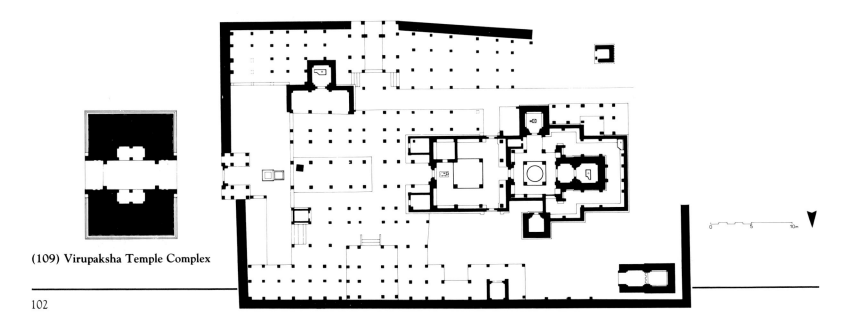

(109) Virupaksha Temple Complex

this area is elevated above the surrounding corridor and faces east onto a large hall. Other palaces nearby are built close together and separated only by narrow alleys. The basements of smaller examples are bounded by plastered earth moldings instead of the more enduring stone.

ZONE OF ROYAL PERFORMANCE

The enclosures in this part of the royal center are larger and more clearly defined than those in the zone of royal residence. The largest enclosure, sometimes identified as the king's palace, lies southeast of the Ramachandra complex. It is entered on the north through a sequence of gateways that leads from the plaza in front of the temple. The enclosure was once filled with structures. In recent years the Archaeological Survey of India has uncovered and restored the masonry foundations and basements of halls and platforms. These include the hundred-columned hall in the northwest corner of the enclosure, the Mahanavami platform in the northeast corner (occupying the highest part of the royal center), and a series of long, narrow halls and monumental baths in the southern part of the enclosure. Aqueducts, wells, and small tanks occur throughout the enclosure, testifying to a complex hydraulic system. Immediately outside the enclosure, near the southeast corner, is the square water pavilion.

Northeast of the Ramachandra complex is another enclosure, often designated as the zenana (or women's quarters) but probably having little to do with the courtly women. More likely, this was the residence of the king or commander of the army. The enclosure is notable for the well-preserved, two-storied pavilion, popularly known as the lotus mahal, which stands in the middle. Nearby are the remains of two palace structures. A rectangular vaulted pavilion stands in the northwest corner, while there are three watchtowers set into the enclosure walls. East of the enclosure is a large open area, probably used for parades, with facing elephant stables, and another structure that may have had a military purpose. A ruined gateway on the west provided access.

HUNDRED-COLUMNED HALL (Figure 110)

This structure probably served as a hall of public audience for the king or his representative. The platform is laid out as a vast square, more than forty meters on each side, defined by basement moldings. Ten rows of ten footing blocks to support massive timber columns, now lost, are set into the plaster floor. Staircases on the west and south lead to one or more vanished upper levels. It is possible that an elevated chamber on the west once looked down on the columned hall.

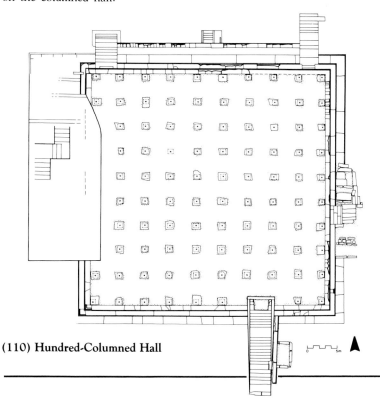

(110) Hundred-Columned Hall

(111) Columned Structures

Two flights of steps flanked by balustrades with spiral designs descend to a plaza on the north side of the hall. Here, two water tanks are set into the ground. A long, monolithic water trough lies nearby.

COLUMNED STRUCTURES AND UNDERGROUND CHAMBER (Figure 111)

Immediately south of the hundred-columned hall are the remains of many smaller square and rectangular columned structures. These possibly housed the activities of the ministers and other elite who surrounded the ruler. The structures are built close together, sometimes even upon one another at different levels, demonstrating a complex history of construction. In between are alleys and open courts, some paved with imported gray-green chlorite or white limestone slabs. Several sculpted limestone pieces were discovered by excavators; these appear to have been taken from a third- or fourth-century Buddhist monument at another site.

In the middle of these structures and courts is a subterranean chamber surrounded by a corridor, possibly an underground treasury. The chamber is fashioned from chlorite slabs reused from a dismantled temple. Further south is a series of long platforms, regularly laid out and separated by narrow alleys. An aqueduct runs along the southern enclosure wall. Elsewhere there are numerous small wells, baths, and water-storage tanks. Excavators have uncovered small plaster sculptures, possibly from the facades of buildings, and stone mortars for pounding grain.

MULTISTORIED PLATFORM (Endpapers, Figures 22-23, 112-113)

This platform is most often named after the Mahanavami festival with which it is associated. The platform stands in the northeast corner of the largest enclosure of the royal center, rising above a granite outcrop, part of which protrudes from beneath the structure. While no traces of foundations for a superstructure are now visible, a wooden tower may have been raised above the platform. Alternatively, a timber pavilion may have been erected temporarily at festival time.

The platform itself is constructed in four successive phases. The first two phases may be assigned to the fourteenth century, coinciding with the period when the royal center was first laid out. They consist of two massive granite basements, one set back above the other. A staircase projects outward on the south side. Relief sculptures cover the stone blocks on the south and east; on the east and north the blocks are partly concealed, due to the later rise in ground level. The carvings here are varied and lively. There are processions of elephants, camels, and horses with riders and attendants, as well as hunting episodes with lions, tigers, and deer. Rows of mounted warriors, footmen with shields and swords, stick bearers, banner-carriers, musicians, entertainers (including male drummers and dancers with pointed beards, sometimes identified as Muslims), and female dancers and musicians are shown. Courtly

(112) Multi storied Platform

(114) Chlorite Tank

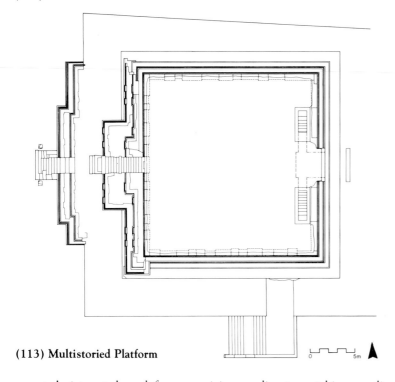

(113) Multistoried Platform

(115) Square Water Pavilion

scenes depict seated royal figures receiving supplicants, watching wrestling matches, and reviewing troops.

The third phase of construction, which dates to the fifteenth century, consists of a series of deeply cut basement moldings. These rest on a base with panels sculpted with processions of animals, dancers, and musicians. The basement creates a vast, square floor area, more than twenty-two meters on each side. Also belonging to this phase is an internal double staircase; this leads up to the top of the platform in the middle of the eastern side. Here, carved processions of animals, dancers, and musicians are joined by hunters on elephants and guardian figures.

The fourth phase, of gray-green chlorite slabs on the west side of the platform, belongs to the sixteenth century. This addition may correspond to the renovation of the throne platform by Krishnadevaraya after his victorious Orissa campaign, an event noted in Domingo Paes's chronicles. The intricate carving of the basement moldings, which are ornamented with niches framing miniature figures, corresponds to features in sixteenth-century temple architecture. A staircase leads to the top of the platform in the middle of the western side.

Southwest of the platform, a rectangular tank with the foundations of a central pavilion and a T-shaped bath have recently been uncovered.

MONUMENTAL TANKS (Figures 46, 47, 114)
The southeast quadrant of the enclosure is occupied by two large tanks, probably ritual bathing places for the ruler and his entourage. One tank has finely worked chlorite steps descending to the water on four sides. The steps are symmetrically arranged to create complex patterns of recessed planes. The other tank forms an immense rectangle raised on an artificial embankment. The interior brick walls of the tank are plaster-lined. Traces of columns indicate a colonnade on four sides. The pavilion on the west is a modern reconstruction. Similarly rebuilt are the aqueduct, raised water channels, and drains in the vicinity.

SQUARE WATER PAVILION (Figures 33, 115-116)
This structure is often referred to as the queens' bath but is also likely to have functioned as a bathing place for the ruler and the male members of the court. The pavilion, which is located outside the previously described enclosure, is surrounded on four sides by a water channel. It presents an austere exterior, since the overhanging eaves and two towers recorded in nineteenth-century photographs are now lost.

The interior is dominated by an open court occupied by a water basin; the stone chute to conduct the water is in situ. The court is surrounded on four

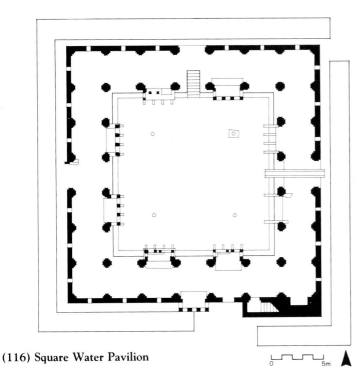

(116) Square Water Pavilion

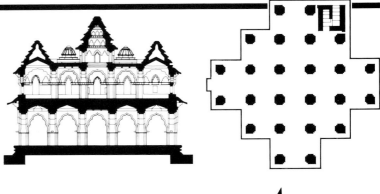

(117) Two-Storied Pavilion, section

(118) Two-Storied Pavilion

sides by an arcade of vaulted bays. Projecting balconies have elevated benches and pointed arched openings supported by corbels. A portion of the parapet with arched openings is preserved above. Traces of delicate plaster decoration with stylized foliate motifs show that the building was provided with an elaborate ornamentation. The vaults roofing the arcade are varied, no two being exactly alike. They, too, were decorated, particularly with plaster geese and parrots. A staircase at the southeast corner of the building ascends to the roof.

TWO-STORIED PAVILION (Figures 20, 117-118)

This best-preserved structure in the zone of royal performance is popularly known as the Lotus Mahal. Despite its fanciful name, the pavilion is likely to have been a residence of the king or his military commander; this is suggested by its proximity to the elephant stables. The building is laid out on a symmetrical plan, with double projections in the middle of each side. An additional bay at the northeast corner is for the staircase tower that provides access to the upper level. Decorative foliate and geometric motifs on the stone basement are carved in flat, Islamic-style relief. The exterior is dominated by large, cusped, arched openings in two or three planes. These openings are surrounded by deeply sculpted plaster bands of stylized foliation and rows of geese. Similarly modeled monster masks are positioned at the tops of the arches; roundels with geometric ornament are placed in the spandrels. Projecting stone brackets once carried stone frames within the openings; these frames repeated the cusped profiles of the arches. Both stories have an overhanging, double-curved eave carried on brackets. The eight projecting bays of the upper level are roofed with pyramidal towers, each a sequence of deeply recessed, eavelike moldings. The capping roof elements are either ribbed or octagonal-domed. The tower over the central bay is raised up to crown the whole composition.

The crudely built staircase tower, which abuts the eave of the pavilion, appears to be a later addition or at least a replacement of an earlier structure. The interiors of both stories have open bays roofed with shallow vaults. The vault is extended upwards in a series of stages above the central bay of the upper level. Traces of original plaster figures remain within the niches here.

PALACES (Figures 119-120)

Two ruined palaces are preserved to the west of the two-storied pavilion. The first is laid out on a complex plan defined by three tiers of basement moldings, richly carved and with traces of paintings. The moldings define a floor area

with projections on the east, south, and west. Access is from the north, where steps are flanked by striding elephant balustrades. Almost nothing is preserved of the square chambers at the highest level of the palace. Stone footings indicate a veranda that extended around the interior rooms and court on the second basement. A covered porch probably also covered the entryway. Traces of walls indicate that the palace once stood within a court.

(119) Palace and Square Watchtower

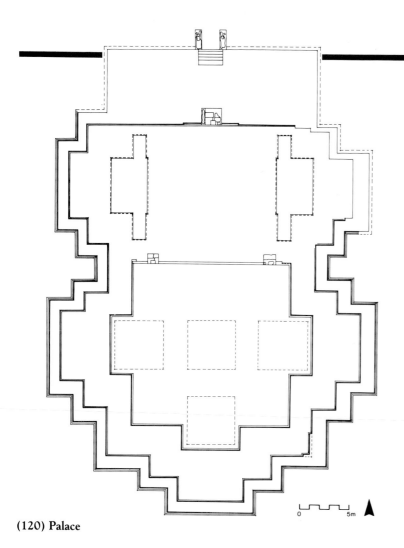

(120) Palace

(121) Vaulted Rectangular Structure

SQUARE AND OCTAGONAL WATCHTOWERS (Figures 17, 25, 54, 122-123)
Three watchtowers are positioned in the walls of the same enclosure, surveying the approaches to the royal center. Of the two square watchtowers in the northern walls, one is preserved to its full height. This consists of an unadorned square shaft containing the staircase. A pavilion at the top has projecting balconies on four sides with arched openings and sheltering eaves. Traces of plasterwork suggest an elaborate ornamentation. The brickwork includes fragments of an ornamental parapet.

The watchtower in the southeast corner of the enclosure has an octagonal shaft. This contains a central, circular staircase surrounded by vaulted chambers, some with arched openings. The upper level has projecting balconies on eight sides, with intermediate openings. Parapet elements above imitate temple towers with miniature vaulted roofs. The summit of the tower has two recessed eavelike moldings and a capping ribbed finial.

The second palace, south of the first, stands in the middle of a rectangular water basin. It is reached by a bridge in the middle of the south side. Fish are sculpted in low relief on the sides of the basin. Traces of walls show that the building may have been surrounded by a colonnade.

VAULTED RECTANGULAR STRUCTURE (Figure 121)
This relatively well-preserved building stands in the northwest corner of the same enclosure as that containing the two-storied pavilion. Though sometimes known as the guards' quarters, this structure may have been a store for guns, cannons, and gunpowder or, alternatively, a gymnasium for the king and male members of the court.

The rectangular building has a plain exterior with only a single opening in the middle of the eastern side. Small ventilation holes are placed high up in the walls, which are overhung by a deep, double-curved eave; the supporting stone rafters are decorated with cobra hoods. The vaulted roof is partly concealed by a pierced masonry parapet with intersecting merlon motifs. The roof is hipped, with angled faces on four sides. The long north-south ridge is raised up and decorated with foliate motifs.

The interior has a raised arcade on four sides that looks down on a central rectangular area. The pointed vault above is carried on eight cusped arches. Shallow vaults roof the bays of the arcade.

(122) Octagonal Watchtower

 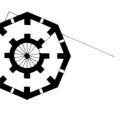 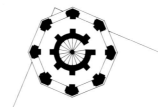 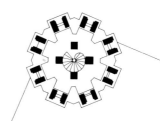

(123) Octagonal Watchtower

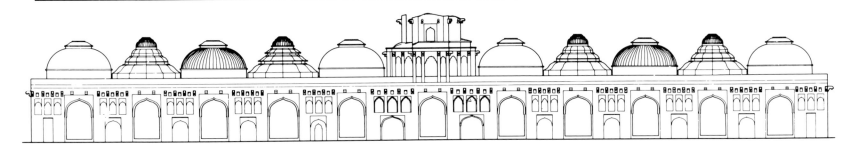

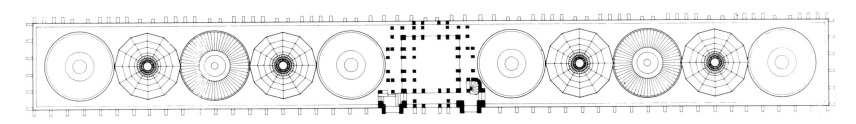

(124) Elephant Stables

ELEPHANT STABLES (Figures 13, 19, 124)
The largest and most monumental courtly structure within the royal center is the elephant stables, which face on a spacious open plaza. The stables consist of eleven square chambers, some connected by doorways, aligned in a long north-south row, with large entrances on the west and small entries on the east. Two staircases in the middle of the building ascend to the roof, where there is a freestanding open chamber.

The exterior of the stables is dominated by the arched openings of the chambers, each flanked by sets of three smaller arched wall recesses. The angled eave at the top has now fallen, but supporting brackets survive. Ten chambers, roofed by alternating domes and vaults of different designs, are symmetrically arranged about the central tower. The domes have alternating plain and fluted exteriors ornamented with bands of merlon motifs. The vaults are built on an unusual twelve-sided plan and are divided into three tiers capped by ribbed roof elements. Though mostly fallen, the central chamber on the roof consists of supporting piers with intermediate arched openings.

The interiors of the chambers have corner-arched squinches supporting domes and vaults. The domes are simple or fluted; the vaults are octagonal or square, with curved ribs. Some domes and vaults are adorned with templelike parapet forms in free-standing brickwork. Others have elaborate friezes of plasterwork.

RECTANGULAR STRUCTURE (Figures 125-126)
This structure faces southward onto the same open plaza as the elephant stables. The rectangular building has an elevated arcade from which there is an excellent view over the plaza. It may, in fact, have been used exactly for the purpose of viewing the activities below. The interior, which consists of a long rectangular court at ground level surrounded by a raised arcade, may have been for martial excercises or sports. The front (south) arcade has steep,

cusped arches once filled with stone frames that repeated the cusped profiles. The interior arcade has unadorned columns supporting pointed arches and shallow vaults.

Dilapidated basements, walls, and stone footings nearby indicate a large, two-storied gateway that provided access to the plaza from a sequence of interlinked courts to the west. On the south side of the plaza is a mound concealing the remains of a structure.

(125) Rectangular Structure

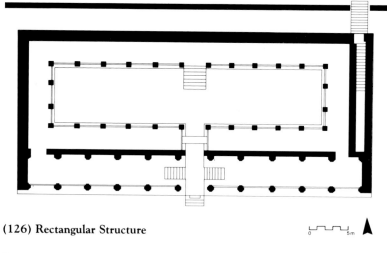

(126) Rectangular Structure

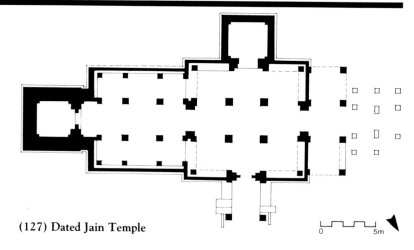

(127) Dated Jain Temple

BEGINNING OF THE NORTHEAST ROAD (Figures 14, 52)

The road that proceeds in a northeast direction from the Ramachandra temple through the royal center begins at a ruined gateway. Only the lower portions of this gateway still stand, but these indicate that the opening was once spanned by a pointed arch.

Both inside and outside the gateway are dilapidated shrines and mandapas, mostly small and modestly decorated structures recently cleared of accumulated earth. Colonnades, a well, and several tanks are also associated with the complex. One shrine east of the gate is contained within a collapsed sixteenth-century hall, the column shafts of which are sculpted with an unusual variety of gods and saints.

ELLAMMA TEMPLE

Further along the northeast road is the Ellamma temple, the only shrine still used for worship in the royal center. The temple, which is partly buried in the ground, is dedicated to a fierce goddess whose image is enshrined in the sanctuary at the end of a long hall. A large reservoir with stone sides is situated to the south, but the steps that once descended to the water have mostly caved in.

MADHAVA TEMPLE COMPLEX (Figure 17)

This complex faces southeast onto the northeast road immediately south of the enclosure containing the two-storied pavilion and ruined palaces. The temple consists of two shrines and associated columned halls. The principal shrine has a sanctuary, antechamber, and columned hall. According to an inscription on a column (SII, IV, no. 248), an image of Madhava was once installed here. Now a large slab carved with a Hanuman image is placed within the hall. The exterior of the sanctuary is severely plain, in contrast with the ornately finished brick tower, which is divided into ascending stories with pilastered niches. The capping roof is hemispherical.

The secondary shrine in the Madhava complex has elaborately carved basement moldings and pilastered walls that now lean dangerously. Only portions of the open mandapa that stood in front of this shrine survive. The columns support carved beams and ceiling slabs.

DATED JAIN TEMPLE AND NEARBY STRUCTURES (Figure 127)

This temple, which faces northwest onto the road, has two square columned halls linked by a doorway. A sanctuary opens off each of the columned halls. The outer hall is entered through two porches. The temple is austere throughout, the only architectural interest being the columns with double capitals and the small Jain figures carved onto the doorway lintels. An inscription in the porch wall, which is dated to 1426 (during the reign of Devaraya II), gives details about the bazaar held in the northeast road (SII, I, no. 153).

Two smaller, dilapidated shrines, dedicated to Shiva and to a Jain savior, face the dated Jain temple from the opposite side of the northeast road. Further along the road is a ruined sanctuary, of which only the porch remains. This has piers carved in the typical sixteenth-century manner with clusters of colonettes and rearing animals. The piers are overhung by deeply curved eaves, now partly fallen.

VAISHNAVA TEMPLE COMPLEX (Figures 56, 128)

This abandoned complex is surrounded by an enclosure wall with a towered gateway giving access from the road on the southeast. The temple itself consists of a sanctuary surrounded on three sides by a passageway; in front is a columned mandapa with side porches. Another connecting porch links the mandapa with the entrance gateway.

The small associated gopura, though partly ruined, is an elaborate sixteenth century structure. It has finely finished basement moldings, pilastered walls, and a brick tower with traces of plaster figures. The temple itself is unusually plain, the only carvings being on the porch and mandapa columns. The multistoried brick tower that rises over the sanctuary was once capped with a hemispherical roof. The courtyard is surrounded by a colonnade, now mostly collapsed.

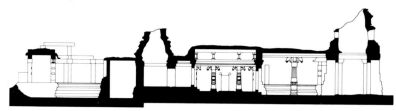

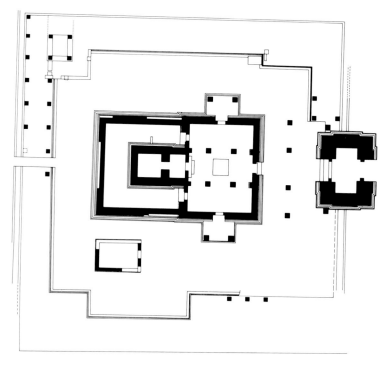

(128) Vaishnava Temple Complex

EAST GATEWAY (Figure 129)

This gateway marks the eastern boundary of the royal center; from here the northeast road enters the urban core on its way to the Islamic quarter. The gateway is approached from the east through a large enclosure created by massive, stone-faced walls. The basement of a ruined shrine is visible inside the enclosure. A completely preserved temple is elevated on the north walls. This small structure has a sanctuary and a square hall with four internal columns; a brick tower rises over the sanctuary.

Masonry platforms with basement moldings line the passageway that leads to the gateway doorway. The walls flanking the doorway have ornamental pilasters and one surviving corbel. One jamb preserved in situ is carved with a guardian brandishing a club. (The other jamb, now displayed in the Archaeological Museum at Kamalapuram, depicts a guardian with a spear.)

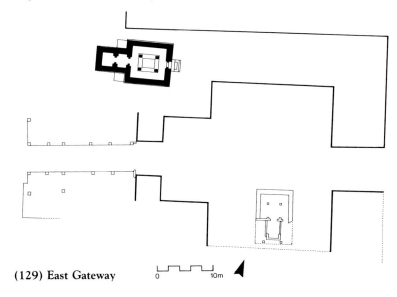

(129) East Gateway 0 10m

SHAIVA TEMPLE COMPLEX (Figure 130)

Located southwest of the enclosures, this complex is one of the largest religious monuments in the royal center. It is sometimes known as the Chandrashekhara temple, even though there is no evidence indicating to which aspect of Shiva the shrine is dedicated. The architectural style suggests an early sixteenth-century date.

The temple stands in a rectangular enclosure, entered in the middle of the east side through a towered gopura. The temple has two sanctuaries, each approached through an antechamber opening off the north and west sides, respectively, of a square, columned mandapa; an open porch adjoins the mandapa on the east. The exterior has a high basement with finely finished moldings and regularly spaced pilasters, some framing niches now devoid of sculptures. Multistoried brick towers rise over the two sanctuaries: one is square with a hemispherical roof, the other rectangular with a vaulted roof. The interior is unadorned, the only decoration being the carvings on the column blocks.

The entrance gopura is relatively small, though well preserved. The three diminishing stories of the brick tower have many plaster figures. The plaster details of the vaulted roof are mostly intact.

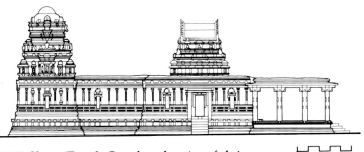

(130) Shaiva Temple Complex, elevation of shrine 0 5m

TIRUVENGALANATHA TEMPLE (Figure 43)

This temple stands immediately north of the Shiva complex. An inscription dated 1554 indicates that the shrine was originally dedicated to Tiruvengalanatha, even though it is sometimes known as the Sarasvati shrine (ARSIE, 1936, no. 337). The small building consists of a north-facing, towered sanctuary and a columned mandapa. The unadorned granite basement and walls contrast with the detailed moldings and fragmentary plaster sculptures of the brick tower. A chlorite pedestal within the sanctuary is empty, but an image of Garuda is carved on the side. The hall columns have carved blocks.

(131) Octagonal Bath

OCTAGONAL BATH AND PALACE (Figure 131)

A short distance northeast of the Tiruvengalanatha temple is an octagonal arcade surrounding a water basin, now empty. In the middle of the basin is a small, stone, octagonal platform, the sides of which have finely finished moldings. In contrast, the rough columns of the arcade have lost their plaster coating. A ruined rectangular structure, originally with three bays, abuts the colonnade to the southwest.

This bath was part of a large palace complex. Immediately north is a high mound out of which rubble walls protrude. These form part of an east-facing palace structure and possess the characteristic sequence of rising floor levels. The palace is set within a rectangular enclosure around which cluster the ruins of several buildings. To the west of the mound stands a small gateway.

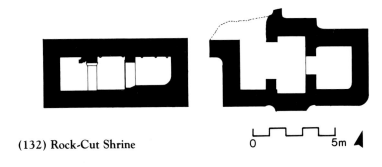

(132) Rock-Cut Shrine 0 5m

ROCK-CUT SHRINE (Figure 132)

North of the octagonal bath is a granite outcrop, the north face of which has an excavated shrine that is the only completely rock-cut monument at Vijayanagara. The shrine consists of a simple, small antechamber, and sanctuary.

South and west of Vijayanagara's urban core, the landscape opens up into a broad, irrigated plain bounded on the west by the Tungabhadra River, on the south by the curving ranges of the Sandur Hills, and on the east by lower granite ridges (Figure 3). Isolated walls still stand, fragmentary remains of the concentric fortifications that protected the urban core on the east, south, and west. In several cases, walls cross low-lying areas to form dams. Water served agricultural and domestic needs and also created marshy ground that was difficult for attackers to cross.

Present-day towns and villages in the plain and on the opposite bank of the Tungabhadra are built on the sites of Vijayanagara-period settlements. Standing and ruined structures at these sites, together with scattered artifacts, provide information about the character of these original suburban centers. The surviving monuments indicate the different religions of Vijayanagara's outlying communities.

KAMALAPURAM

This village is located immediately south of the urban core. A fort with rounded bastions, only part of which dates from the Vijayanagara era, once stood in the middle of the village. This has been mostly demolished, with only a single gateway remaining. A small Shiva temple stands within the fort, while another temple nearby has been converted into a traveler's bungalow.

South of the village is a large, Vijayanagara-period reservoir. A dam on the north, over which the modern road now runs, forms part of an arc of fortifications extending to the east and west of the village. Channels leading from this reservoir once conducted water to the royal center; they still feed the irrigated valley.

The Archaeological Museum is located at Kamalapuram. This houses an open-air model of Vijayanagara that gives the best possible idea of the layout of the site. The galleries also display coins, inscriptions, and isolated sculptures that have been removed from monuments. The carvings depict various deities. Architectural pieces include balustrades and columns. Numerous hero stones, commemorating the death of heroes in battle, are placed in the surrounding yard.

PATTABHIRAMA TEMPLE COMPLEX (Figures 53, 133-134)

This large complex is situated northeast of Kamalapuram, only a short distance from the domed gateway that provides access to the southeast part of the urban core. Among the four inscriptions on the temple recording grants of land or money is one dated 1539, during the reign of Achyutadevaraya. The deity mentioned in these inscriptions is Raghunatha.

The complex consists of the principal temple, standing in the middle of a vast rectangular enclosure, with a smaller, minor shrine to the northwest. A columned hall is positioned against the enclosure wall south of the temple. The principal entrance is a towered gopura on the east with a smaller gateway on the south.

The temple has a sanctuary surrounded on three sides by a passageway. To the east there are a columned mandapa with porches on the north and south and a large open mandapa. The architectural style is impressive though austere. The low exterior is dominated by the long lines of the basement and cornice moldings; the walls have pilasters, some framing empty niches. The multistoried brick tower is capped with a hemispherical roof. The outer columns of the open mandapa are fashioned as piers, with rearing yalis in the middle of each side and groups of colonettes clustering around a central shaft at the corners. There is no parapet preserved above the overhanging eave.

The minor shrine is similar in style, but the tower over the sanctuary is of the vaulted type on a rectangular plan. The columned hall against the southern enclosure wall has elegant columns with colonettes on the periphery. The raised floor level at the rear (south) is somewhat dilapidated. The basement and walls on the east and west sides of the hall are similar to those of the temple.

Despite the deterioration of its brickwork, the eastern gopura preserves

much of its original character. The lower granite portion has deeply cut basement moldings and pilastered walls. Carved jambs are placed within the walkway. The pyramidal tower rises in five ascending but diminishing stories, with openings in the middle of the long sides. There is almost no surviving plasterwork. The tower is capped with an enlarged, vaulted roof.

(133) Pattabhirama Temple Complex

134) Pattabhirama Temple Complex

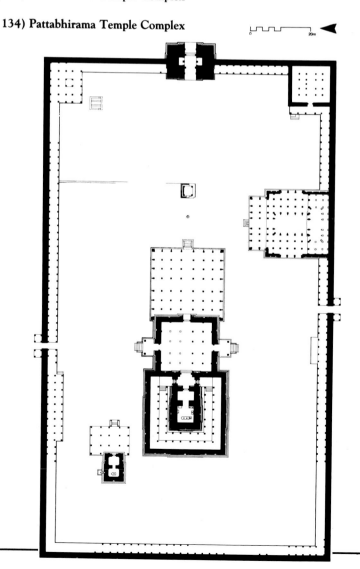

A short distance east of the complex is an overgrown reservoir surrounded by a colonnade. A portion of the Kamalapuram fortification walls with gateways survives further to the east. Several small shrines stand inside the Penukonda gateway, which is named in an inscription within one of the shrines (SII, IV, no. 245).

MALPANNAGUDI (Figures 59, 135-136)
This village is situated on the road linking Hampi and Kamalapuram with the town of Hospet. Malpannagudi was evidently a settlement of some importance during Vijayanagara times, as two gateways still stand at either end of the village. The eastern gateway once formed part of a line of fortifications that included a large reservoir to the southeast of the town. The gateways are simple, open structures with horizontal roof slabs. One example now serves to store the temple chariot.

The only Vijayanagara-period monument within the village is the Mallikarjuna temple. This stands within a square compound, fortified in later times and entered on the west through a gopura facing on the main road. The sanctuary is roofed with a brick tower having a hemispherical roof. The adjoining mandapa has an elaborate parapet with plaster figures; similar figures are found on the tops of the enclosure walls.

An inscription on a slab lying in front of the temple is dated 1412; it mentions the construction of a well (ARSIE, 1904, no. 25). In all likelihood, this is the well located about five hundred meters southwest of the village beside the Hospet road. The well has an octagonal shaft, surrounded by a vaulted arcade with arched openings. The water is approached by a long flight of steps.

(137) Kadirampuram, Tomb

KADIRAMPURAM (Figures 32, 137)
This village is located west of the urban core. That a Muslim community once lived here is indicated by two tombs situated on the outskirts of the village. The larger tomb now lacks a dome. It consists of a square chamber, the outer walls of which have arched recesses in two tiers. The interior has squinches with pointed arches. The smaller tomb preserves its dome. The outer walls have pointed arched recesses and a parapet of merlons. Both tombs may be dated to the early fifteenth century and are comparable to contemporary Bahmani architecture.

ANANTASHAYANA TEMPLE (Figures 60, 138-139)
This monument is situated about 1.5 kilometers northwest of Hospet beside the road leading towards Hampi and Kamalapuram. The modern village of Anantasayanagudi that surrounds the temple is named after it. An inscription dated to 1524 states that the shrine was erected by Krishnadevaraya (ARSIE, 1922, no. 683). The temple stands in a walled compound entered on the west through a large gopura, of which only the lower granite portions remain.

The temple itself consists of a columned mandapa, narrow antechamber, and rectangular sanctuary linked by three doorways. The long pedestal within the sanctuary was intended for an image of a reclining Vishnu, perhaps fash-

(135) Malpannagudi, Well

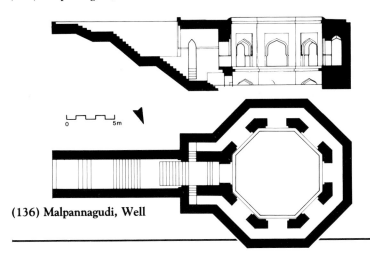

(136) Malpannagudi, Well

(138) Anantashayana Temple

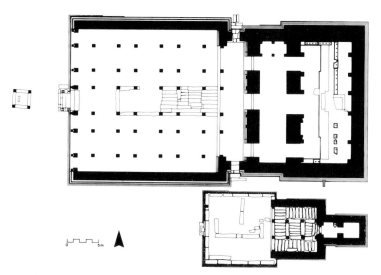

(139) Anantashayana Temple

ioned in plaster-covered brickwork, of which nothing now remains. The sanctuary is roofed with a high, pointed-arched vault. On the exterior this rises as a brick tower of two stories with niches containing plaster figures. The tower has part-circular ends carried up into the capping curved vault. The mandapa is open on the front (west), where piers have single colonettes; the other columns are enlivened with carved blocks. The parapet over the double-curved eave has been much restored. A smaller, minor shrine is situated to the southeast.

HOSPET (Figure 140)

This is the largest town in the vicinity of the Vijayanagara site - a center for local transport, a major market, and the point of arrival for most pilgrims and tourists to Hampi and the ruins. The Tungabhadra Hydroelectric Dam, another attraction, is situated only a short distance southwest of the town. In the early sixteenth century Krishnadevaraya laid out a new residence in the vicinity of Hospet, naming it after one of his queens. Today, nothing survives of this royal suburb.

Two tombs in the southern part of Hospet, however, suggest the presence of a Muslim community dating back to the Vijayanagara period. One of these tombs is now ruined, but it is similar to the domeless example at Kadirampuram, having arched recesses on the facade and arched squinches inside. The other example, dome intact, was built no earlier than the sixteenth century. It has an elaborate parapet with merlon motifs.

Evidence of extensive hydraulic projects in the Hospet area are visible to the south of the town, where a massive earthen wall bridges the gap between two hills. A modern road runs over the dam.

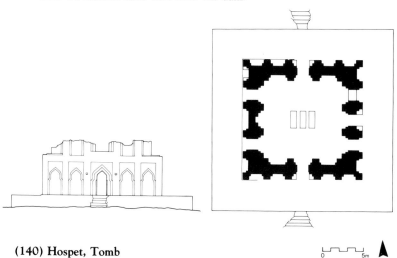

(140) Hospet, Tomb

ANEGONDI (Figures 8, 61, 141-142)

The town of Anegondi is situated on the bank of the Tungabhadra opposite to Vijayanagara at a point where the river turns northward. The town has a longer history than Vijayanagara, having been an important habitation and fort in earlier times. After the abandonment of Vijayanagara, Anegondi was resettled by members of a royal family that claimed direct descent from the Vijayanagara kings. The earliest visitors to Vijayanagara stayed in Anegondi, then the only habitation in the vicinity.

Anegondi is surrounded by a circuit of fortifications with gateways on the north and south. These gateways are early structures, probably dating from the fourteenth century, judging from the massive columns and horizontal roof slabs. A later gateway with part-circular bastions probably belongs to the seventeenth century. The eastern walls of the town follow the riverbank, where there are long stone steps for bathing. Numerous religious and courtly monuments still stand within the town; other early buildings either have been incorporated into later structures or have collapsed.

The earliest-dated temple in Anegondi is a Jain shrine that, according to one reading of an inscription found there, was erected in 1342 during the period of Harihara I (ARIE, 1958-9, no. B678). The temple presents a sequence of porch, mandapa, and sanctuary, all built in unadorned, massive masonry. The tower over the sanctuary is a pyramid of receding horizontal moldings. Immediately in front (east) of the temple is a fragmentary structure with an elaborate doorway framed by pierced stone screens, all executed in chlorite. This is all that remains of a Late Chalukya temple dating from the eleventh or twelfth century.

In the middle of the town is an open square onto which opens the east-facing Ranganatha temple. This typical sixteenth-century complex has two enclosures linked by a moderate-sized gopura with a pyramidal brick tower. The temple itself is approached through an open mandapa, the outer columns of which are elaborate. The sanctuary and adjoining closed mandapa are modest structures, possibly dating back to the fourteenth century.

Opposite the temple, facing west onto the town square, is the courtly structure known as the Gagan Mahal. This was probably built no earlier than the seventeenth century and is now used as the headquarters for the local town council. The pavilion is a long, rectangular building with vaulted chambers at the upper level. Balconies projecting outward from these chambers have pointed-arched openings and overhanging eaves; traces of plaster decoration still survive. The exterior is dominated by three towers in a row, each with ascending tiers of eavelike moldings and capping domelike roofs. An octagonal staircase adjoining the building at its southern end provides access to the roof. The staircase has a tower capped with a fluted, domed roof.

(141) Anegondi, Gagan Mahal

(142) Anegondi, Watchtowers

A group of small shrines, facing east towards the river, is located in the southeastern part of the town. These are mostly fourteenth- and fifteenth-century structures of small proportions with undecorated exteriors. One unusual building has shrines on two levels. Gateways lead to steps, which then descend to the water.

A dilapidated mandapa stands outside the town walls near the path that links the southern gate of the town with the river crossing to Vijayanagara. The hall is partly built of reused chlorite columns having delicately carved circular shafts and capitals in the typical Late Chalukya manner. Paintings once covered the ceiling of the hall, but only the barest fragments remain. A brick tower rises over the middle of the hall, which is here raised to two stories.

The hill west of the town is a fortified citadel surrounded by massive walls. Gateways guard the approaches from the south and east; one is flanked by part-circular bastions with parapets of merlons above. A balcony with pointed arched openings concealing a raised chamber projects over the doorway.

Part of the citadel encloses a shallow valley with a number of structures. These include circular masonry granaries, a ruined courtly pavilion with an internal water basin, tanks, and wells. Elsewhere in the citadel there is a long rectangular structure with a central line of columns, possibly the barracks.

A royal funerary monument stands on an outcrop below the eastern walls. Templelike in form, it probably dates to the nineteenth century. Immediately underneath the western walls of the citadel are two ponds overlooked by a small goddess temple and a Shiva shrine; this is the site of the Pampa Sarovar. A cavern nearby is associated with Shabari. Beneath the northern slope of the citadel is a temple with a towered gateway built between the rocks. This leads to a shrine that extends underneath an overhanging ledge.

Another line of fortifications extends northeast of the town, following the bank of the Tungabhadra. A complex of walls and gateways, extending more than one kilometer north of Anegondi, represents the northernmost limit of the Vijayanagara site. The fortifications are entered through a large gateway. Several small shrines face the road that leads from Anegondi to these outer walls.

APPENDICES

LIST OF KINGS AT VIJAYANAGARA

Sangama Dynasty 1336-1485
Harihara I, 1336-1354/5
Bukka I, 1354/5-1377
Harihara II, 1377-1404
Virupaksha I and Bukka II, 1404-1406
Devaraya I, 1406-1422
Vijaya I, 1422-1424
Devaraya II, 1424-1446
Mallikarjuna, 1446-1465
Virupaksha II, 1465-1485

Saluva Dynasty, 1485-1506
Saluva Narasimha, 1485-1492
Immadi Narasimha, 1492-1506

Tuluva Dynasty, 1506-1570
Vira Narasimha, 1506-1509
Krishnadevaraya, 1510-1529
Achyutadevaraya, 1529-1542
Venkata I, 1542
Sadashiva, 1542-1570

GLOSSARY

Architectural Terms

ashram, residence of a holy man

balustrade, sidepiece of a staircase

barbican, protective outer enclosure of a gateway

barrel vault, vault with a circular or part-circular profile

basement, lower part of the wall beneath the floor, usually divided into moldings

bastion, projecting tower in fortification walls

bracket, projecting block supporting a balcony or eave

chlorite, gray-green stone not found at Vijayanagara

colonette, miniature column

corbel, projecting block

cornice, horizontal band

cusped arch, having part-circular profiles or lobes

dharmashala, a place of prayer or meditation

domelike, having the appearance of a dome, but generally constructed in solid masonry

eave, overhang, usually with a double-curved profile

finial, capping piece

fluted, fluting, concave or convex designs in domes or vaults

foliate, foliation, design based on plant forms

footing, block to support a column

frieze, horizontal row of carvings

gable, triangular end of roof

garbhagriha, temple sanctuary

ghat, bathing place, usually with steps, also hill leading down to the ocean

gopura, towered entrance to a temple

hip, angled, triangular part of a roof

infill wall, thin wall bearing little or no load

jamb, sides of a doorway

kalyana mandapa, hall for the ritual marriage ceremony of the god and goddess

lintel, beam over a doorway

mandapa, columned hall, often attached to a temple sanctuary

matha, monastery

merlon, battlement with a curved top, often used ornamentally for a parapet or a cornice

mihrab, prayer niche in a mosque indicating the direction of Mecca

mortar, stone for grinding grain

niche, wall recess, usually for a sculpture

parapet, wall above the eave concealing the roof

pier, massive, vertical support or short wall

pilaster, narrow flat column forming part of the wall fabric

plinth, supporting basement or pedestal

sanctuary, small square or rectangular chamber housing the image or emblem of the deity to which the temple is dedicated

squinch, archlike supporting element beneath a dome

superstructure, tower

tank, reservoir or dam

vault, curved or angled roof over a bay

Glossary of Indian Deities and Religious Terms

Adinarayana, epithet of Vishnu

Agastya, sage of the gods

Anantashayana, name of Vishnu when reclining on the serpent Shesha

Balakrishna, Krishna as a crawling infant

Bhima, a hero of the Mahabaharata

Bhudevi, female consort of Vishnu

Bhuvaneshvari, name of Parvati

Brahma, the god of creation, believed to rule over the center of the mandala

chakra, disklike weapon associated with Vishnu

Chandrashekhara, name of Shiva

darshana, auspicious view of a god or goddess that forms the climax of devotional rites

Durga, fierce goddess

Ellamma, name of Kali

Ganesha, elephant-headed god sometimes considered a son of Shiva

Garuda, eagle mount of Vishnu

Hanuman, monkey hero of the Ramayana epic; devotee of Rama

Indra, king of the gods

Jambavan, king of the bears who assisted Rama

Kali, fierce and terrifying goddess associated with Shiva

Kodandarama, name of Rama with the bow

Krishna, popular god, an incarnation of Vishnu

Lakshmana, brother of Rama in the Ramayana epic

Lakshmi, female consort of Vishnu

linga, phallic emblem representing the procreative power of Shiva

Madhava, name of Vishnu

Mahabaharata, celebrated Hindu epic

Mahanavami, festival of nine nights in which Rama worshiped Durga

Mahisha, buffalo demon killed by Durga

makara, mythical aquatic monster

Mallikarjuna, name of Shiva

mandala, magical diagram representing the structure of the universe

Manmatha, god of love

Matanga, divine sage in the Ramayana epic, also father of Pampa

Matali, charioteer of Rama

Nandi, bull mount of Shiva

Narasimha, fierce, lion-headed incarnation of Vishnu

Pampa, indigenous goddess of the Tungabhadra valley; identified with Parvati

Pampapati, lord of Pampa, name of Virupaksha

Parvati, female consort of Shiva

Pattabhirama, name of crowned Rama

pradakshina, clockwise circumambulation of a divine or royal person

Purandara Dasa, a sixteenth-century Vaishnava poet and saint

Raghunatha, a name of Rama

Rakshasas, demon army of Ravana

Rama, divine hero of the Ramayana epic; an incarnation of Vishnu

Ramachandra, a name of Rama

Ramanuja, a Vaishnava philosopher and teacher

Ramayana, epic story of Rama

Ranganatha, reclining form of Vishnu

Ravana, king of the demons who abducted Sita in the Ramayana epic

Sarasvati, goddess of music and knowledge

Shabari, untouchable woman who fed Rama

Shaiva, pertaining to the cult of Shiva

shastra, treatise on traditional law that includes information on temple rites, art, architecture, kingship, and myth

Shesha, serpent mount of Vishnu

Shiva, major god of Hinduism

Sita, wife of Rama in the Ramayana epic

Subrahmanya, son of Shiva, commander of the celestial army

Sudarshana, personified disk emblem of Vishnu

Sugriva, monkey king who helped Rama in the Ramayana epic

Tiruvengalanatha, name of Vishnu, worshiped at Tirumala

Vaishnava, pertaining to the cult of Vishnu

Vali, monkey king killed by Rama in the Ramayana epic

Varaha, boar-headed incarnation of Vishnu

Venkateshvara, name of Vishnu, worshiped at Tirumala

Vidyaranya, sage who advised the early Vijayanagara kings

Virabhadra, a fierce form of Shiva

Virupaksha, name of Shiva at Hampi

Vishnu, major god known in various incarnations including Narasimha, Krishna, and Rama

Vithala, name of Vishnu

yali, mythical, lionlike beast

SELECTED BIBLIOGRAPHY

Abbreviations

ARSIE, Annual Report on South Indian Epigraphy, Madras.

ARIE, Annual Report on Indian Epigraphy, Madras.

EI, Epigraphia Indica, Calcutta.

SII, South Indian Inscriptions, Madras.

VPR, Vijayanagara: Progress of Research, editor, M. S. Nagaraja Rao, Mysore, Directorate of Archaeology and Museums.

Monographs and Articles

Dallapiccola, A. L., editor, Vijayanagara, City and Empire: New Currents of Research, Stuttgart, 1985.

Dallapiccola, A. L., J. M. Fritz, G. Michell, and S. Rajasekhara, The Ramachandra Temple at Vijayanagara, New Delhi, 1991.

Devakunjari, D., Hampi, New Delhi, Archaeological Survey of India, 1970.

Fergusson, J., and P. Meadows Taylor, Architecture in Dharwar and Mysore, London, 1866.

Filliozat, P.-S., and V. Filliozat, Hampi-Vijayanagar: The Temple of Vithala, New Delhi,

Sitaram Bhartia Institute of Scientific Research, 1988.

Filliozat, V., "The Town Planning of Vijayanagara," Art and Archaeology Research Papers, XIV (1978), pp. 54-64.

Fritz, J. M., "Vijayanagara: Authority and Meaning of a South Indian Imperial Capital," American Anthropologist, 88/1 (1986), pp. 44-55.

Fritz, J. M., and G. Michell, "Interpreting the Plan of a Medieval Hindu Capital: Vijayanagara," World Archaeology, 19/1 (1987), pp. 105-129.

———, "Window on the Past," Archaeology 42/5 (September/October, 1989), pp. 40-47.

Fritz, J. M., G. Michell, and M. S. Nagaraja Rao, Where Kings and Gods Meet: The Royal Centre at Vijayanagara, Tucson, 1985.

———, "Vijayanagara: City of Victory," World Archaeology, 39/2 (March/April, 1986), pp. 22-29.

Hampi: Heritage Conservation and Development Plan, Ahmedabad, National Institute of Design, [1989].

Heras, H., The Aravidu Dynasty of Vijayanagara, Madras, 1927.

———, "The Prison of Emperor Sadasiva Raya," Indian Antiquary, 40 (1931), pp. 23-25.

Indian Archaeology, 1984-85—A Review, New Delhi, Archaeological Survey of India, 1987, pp. 25-29.

Krishnaswami Aiyangar, S., Sources of Vijayanagara History, Madras, 1919.

———, editor, Vijayanagara Sexcentenary Commemoration Volume, Dharwar, 1936.

Longhurst, A. H., Hampi Ruins, Described and Illustrated, London, 1917.

Mahalingam, T. V., Administration and Social Life under Vijayanagara, Madras, 1975.

Michell, G., "Vijayanagara: City of Victory," History Today, XXXII (1982), pp. 38-42.

———, Architectural Inventory of the Urban Core at Vijayanagara, 2 vols., Mysore, Directorate of Archaeology and Museums, 1990.

———, The Vijayanagara Courtly Style: Incorporation and Synthesis in the Royal Architecture of Southern India, 15th–17th Centuries, New Delhi, 1991.

Michell, G., and V. Filliozat, *Splendours of the Vijayanagara Empire*, Bombay, Marg, 1981.

Nagaraja Rao, M. S., editor, *Vijayanagara through the eyes of Alexander J. Greenlaw 1856, and John Gollings 1983*, Mysore, Directorate of Archaeology and Museums, 1988.

Nilakanta Sastri, K. A., and N. Venkataramanayya, *Further Sources of Vijayanagara History*, Madras, 1946.

Rajasekhara, S., *Masterpieces of Vijayanagara Art*, Bombay, 1983.

Rea, A. "Vijayanagara," *Christian College Magazine*, (1886-87), pp. 428-436, 502-509.

Saletore, B. A., *Social and Political Life in the Vijayanagara Empire*, Madras, 1934.

Sewell, R., *A Forgotten Empire*, London, 1900.

Sherwani, H. K., and P. M. Joshi, editors, *History of Medieval Deccan (1295-1724)*, Hyderabad, 1973-74.

Sinopoli, C., *Pots and Palaces: The Earthenware Ceramics of the Noblemen's Quarters at Vijayanagara*, New Delhi, 1991.

Stein, B., "Mahanavami: Medieval and Modern Kingly Ritual in South India," in

Essays on Gupta Culture, editor, B. L. Smith, Delhi, 1983, pp. 67-90.

———, *The Vijayanagara Kingdom*, Cambridge, 1990.

Verghese, A., *Religious Traditions in the City of Vijayanagara prior to 1565 A. D. (Based on a Study of the Monuments)*, Ph.D. thesis, Bombay, Wilson College, Department of History, 1989.

Watson, A., *The War of the Goldsmith's Daughter*, London, 1964.

INDEX